Oldies' Guide to the Millennial World

Oldies' Guide to the Millennial World

Katy McEwen

LOST
THE
PLOT

A Lost the Plot book, first published in 2020 by Pantera Press Pty Limited
www.PanteraPress.com

Please send all permission queries to:
Pantera Press, P.O. Box 1989, Neutral Bay, NSW, Australia 2089 or
info@PanteraPress.com

A Cataloguing-in-Publication entry for this book is available from the National Library of Australia.
ISBN 978-1-925700-40-4 (Paperback)

Cover design, cover illustrations and internal illustrations: Ngaio Parr
Internal design: Elysia Clapin
Publisher: Martin Green
Editor: Anne Reilly
Proofreaders: Anna Blackie and Lucy Bell
Author photo: Lucy Bell
Printed and bound in Shenzhen Jinhao Colour Printing

Pantera Press policy is to use papers that are natural, renewable and recyclable products made from wood grown in sustainable forests. The logging and manufacturing processes are expected to conform to the environmental regulations of the country of origin.

To my three favourite Millennials: Rach, Matt and Dom.

The future is in good hands xxx

Society Technology Platform

New Concept Lifestyle

Introduction

GENERATIONS seem to be a big deal. Not sure you want to be defined by your year of birth? Aren't we all unique? Yes, of course. Then again, how do you explain kale, quinoa and smashed avocado to someone who grew up on grilled lamb chops and frozen peas?

There's no doubt that world events, developments in technology, and economic and social shifts affect a person's world view, tastes, attitudes and expectations. There are people called demographers who study all that. The consensus is that we can usually relate to individuals born around the same time as us as we have shared influences, and these become a kind of shared language – even if we have different personalities, politics and private experiences.

'MILLENNIALS ARE THE "KEEP YOUR OPTIONS OPEN" GENERATION BECAUSE THEY'VE HAD TO BE.'

Hugh Mackay, social researcher and writer

The trick is learning how to communicate with people who *aren't* born around the same time as us.

In this era of rapid change, it's easy to feel out of touch with how people of different generations speak, and to understand their attitudes and values.

Oldies' Guide to the Millennial World is a quick reference for anyone who's feeling a little out of date with it all and wants a simple crash course.

The *Macquarie Dictionary* defines 'generation' as 'the whole body of individuals born about the same time'. Somehow different generations have acquired nicknames for reference. These naming conventions probably started with the Baby Boomer phenomenon, with the surge of births at the end of the Second World War. There was then a clear and dramatic drop in the birth rate in 1964.

Broadly speaking, people born between 1965 and 1979 came to be known as Generation X, and those born between 1980 and 1995 came to be known as Generation Y, or more colloquially, Millennials.

This is an exciting group. Growing up with a constantly changing array of technology at their fingertips, Millennials have had to devise new ways of relating to each other – and coping with the burden of 24/7 connectivity. According to Patrick Struebi, Millennials have 'an urgent, enthusiastic desire to find new solutions to the world's most pressing problems.'[1] It's definitely worth the effort to figure out what they're speaking about and what they have to say.

'REMEMBER WHEN WE CRIED AS KIDS AND OUR PARENTS SAID, "I'LL GIVE YOU SOMETHING TO CRY ABOUT"?
WE THOUGHT THEY WERE GOING TO HIT US BUT INSTEAD THEY DESTROYED THE HOUSING MARKET, QUADRUPLED COLLEGE TUITION, AND MELTED
THE ICE CAPS.'

Imagine @Funny_Imagine on Twitter

Millennials

INITIALLY, the term 'Millennial' referred specifically to the high school graduating class of the new millennium – which meant those born around 1982.[1] But it has come to replace the term 'Gen Y' and includes the generation born between 1980 and 1995, give or take. In other words, Millennials were the teenagers of the 2000s.

FUN FACT

MILLENNIALS ARE SOMETIMES REFERRED TO AS 'ECHO BOOMERS' BECAUSE THEY'RE OFTEN THE CHILDREN OF BABY BOOMERS.

They've grown up in the shadow of the 9/11 terrorist attacks in 2001 and the resulting cultural atmosphere and social upheaval that has had a significant influence on their young adulthood. The daily life of Millennials is also dominated by digital connectivity. Via smartphones, they are interacting and organising their lives on social media and sharing memes.

What attitudes and behaviours set Millennials apart from other generations? They've had a pretty bad rap, labelled by the media as 'me, me, me'[2] – self-obsessed, selfish, assertive and entitled. They're regarded as the polar opposite of the grounded, sensible Baby Boomers. Much is made of how Millennials behave when they reach adulthood. Where earlier generations have typically settled down – got married, had kids and bought real estate – for Millennials that isn't happening.

Why aren't they hitting the traditional benchmarks? While in some cases the economics are working against them, often Millennials don't find these benchmarks relevant to them. They're just not interested.

'NOT ALL MILLENNIALS THINK ALIKE. A DEMOGRAPHIC IS NOT A PSYCHOGRAPHIC.'

Andy Dunn, CEO and co-founder of online apparel retailer Bonobos

TECHNOLOGY

The World Wide Web

THE bedrock on which the Millennials' digital world is built was being created at the same time they were. Since the 1960s, researchers and government departments had been refining ways to communicate by computer, linking computers to networks through an 'internet'. In 1989, computer scientist Tim Berners-Lee developed a system whereby his computer could look up publicly available information on other people's computers, which he named the World Wide Web (this is the origin of the www in web addresses).

Similar ideas were being explored by other software engineers at that time, but the advantage of Berners-Lee's method was that it was quick, simple and free. Around the world, people began publishing information they wanted to share, and using the internet to surf the web – to follow their noses and click on all sorts of websites.

FUN FACT

THE WORLD WIDE WEB WAS ALMOST CALLED 'INFORMATION MESH' OR 'THE INFORMATION MINE' OR 'MINE OF INFORMATION'.

While for Baby Boomers and Gen-Xers, using the web involved considerable learning, Millennials grew up with it, which is why they were dubbed 'digital natives'.

Even digital natives with no technical understanding of the internet are great at using it efficiently. They have a natural intuition about it and are street smart about what to click (and not click), how menus work and so on. They have a large vocabulary for the ever-expanding visual and interactive realm of technology and an instinctive ability to navigate the interfaces of computers and smartphones. They can also find solutions to digital problems more quickly and efficiently than the 'digital migrants' of the Baby-Boomer and Gen-X eras.

This intrinsic understanding of all things digital is a central element of why Millennials think about and do things differently. The influence that technology has on their lives is enormous and has widespread ramifications on their attitudes and lifestyles.

'THE WEB AS I ENVISAGED IT, WE HAVE NOT SEEN IT YET. THE FUTURE IS STILL SO MUCH BIGGER THAN THE PAST.'

Tim Berners-Lee, inventor of the World Wide Web

Smartphones

KEY to the everyday lives of Millennials is the existence of portable and powerful electronic devices that can fit in your pocket and connect you to the world. Originally, these were mobile phones that offered simple calls plus a few additional features such as games. Separate devices, like the iPod, made an increasingly wide selection of music accessible. As computing power became cheaper and cheaper, the capability of all these devices grew exponentially, and features such as cameras and music players were integrated into phones.

Then came the killer combination of effective data connections, lightweight and long-lasting batteries, and touchscreens: the smartphone was born. Not only could you text and call, but you could now connect instantly to a much wider source of information – the internet.

As if that wasn't mind-blowing enough, software developers started making all kinds of exciting applications, or apps, specially for mobile devices. These optional add-ons – some free, and some not, but many available for less than a dollar – provide users with a dizzying array of enhancements. No matter your requirement – whether you want a built-in calculator, magnifying glass or translation tool, or your interest is games, news, weather or the stockmarket – there's an app for that. And it's only a few clicks or taps away.

It was the Apple iPhone that paved the way and was responsible for the main cultural transition, although the free-to-use Android operating system has since gained a large share of the smartphone market.

With the widespread adoption of the smartphone, the majority of users are accustomed to being connected to the internet 24/7. In turn, this has driven the expansion of platforms and apps like Facebook and Instagram.

The symbiosis of the smartphone and the internet has been transformative. In a generation, teenagers went from having to be at home on a static phone line in order to contact a friend to being able to pull a smartphone out of their pocket and respond immediately. This instant connection, irrespective of location or time of day, means that the default of a Millennial is to be online constantly and available at all times.

'I FEEL ABOUT MY PHONE THE WAY HORROR-MOVIE VENTRILOQUISTS FEEL ABOUT THEIR DUMMIES: IT'S SMARTER THAN ME, BETTER THAN ME, AND I WILL KILL ANYONE WHO COMES BETWEEN US.'

Colson Whitehead, The Noble Hustle: Poker, Beef Jerky & Death

---

Facebook

TYLER AND CAMERON WINKLEVOSS, WHO CLAIM TO HAVE ORIGINALLY ESTABLISHED THE IDEA FOR FACEBOOK, ARE NOW WORTH AROUND AU$1.3 BILLION. FACEBOOK'S FOUNDER, MARK ZUCKERBERG, IS WORTH OVER AU$70 BILLION.

ONCE the World Wide Web was running smoothly, it was seen that a valuable next step would be for people to be able to use the medium to communicate with each other. Take a bow social media! Suddenly, people were opening accounts on social networking websites such as MySpace, which dominated between 2005 and 2008. Among the most pervasive of these networks are Facebook, Reddit and LinkedIn. It's hard to remember a time when they weren't an integral part of so many lives.

Facebook first appeared in the USA in 2004 as a website exclusively for college students at Harvard. It quickly morphed and spread to other Ivy League universities, and then even more widely. It was the vision of co-founder, now CEO, Mark Zuckerberg to build up webs of connections – Facebook friends, also known as 'social networks' – between individuals, and to make their profiles and news publicly shareable and available. Facebook has since expanded into a complete social media platform. Not only does it allow for status updates and the sharing of photos, but its users can keep track of what others are doing, message individuals directly, plan events, organise groups and engage with organisations. It is now one of the three internet giants, along with Google and Amazon.

People use Facebook in numbers that are eye popping. According to a 2018 article from *The New Yorker* magazine, more than 2.2 billion people, about a third of humanity, log on at least once a month.[1]

Different generations use Facebook in different ways. Millennials tend to log on to Facebook to organise their social lives – invitations to get-togethers are issued via Facebook rather than via individual messages – so they can't afford not to be part of it. Facebook is cleverly designed to make users spend as much time as possible there. While the news feed will include the most recent updates from your contacts, you're also directly fed more general news and, of course, a large swathe of advertising. It's the advertising that has made Facebook's founders incredibly wealthy.

The establishment of Facebook's news feed, and its rise as an information channel, has profoundly changed the media landscape. Facebook has stolen attention away from traditional news feeds, especially for Millennials. Content delivered by the site can have a huge influence on the lives of Millennials.[2]

Facebook has come under fire over some of its practices relating to online privacy. People are suspicious of its monopolistic position and the fact that it collects huge amounts of personal data, which in the past has been exploited commercially. For instance, the data of tens of millions of Facebook users was obtained by Cambridge Analytica, a company associated with manipulating voter behaviour, which was subsequently hired by Donald Trump during the 2016 US election. This not only undermined the trust of Facebook users, but also attracted the attention of regulators – so change might well be in the air.

'FACEBOOK WAS NOT ORIGINALLY CREATED TO BE A COMPANY. IT WAS BUILT TO ACCOMPLISH A SOCIAL MISSION – TO MAKE THE WORLD MORE OPEN AND CONNECTED.'

Mark Zuckerberg, Facebook CEO and co-founder

Instagram

WHILE Facebook was establishing itself as both a news feed and means of social connection, two Millennials who met as software students at Stanford University – Kevin Systrom and Mike Krieger – spotted a gap in the social-networking market. In 2010, they released an app that focused on the rapid sharing, also known as 'posting', of photos. This new visual mode of communication was an instant hit.

Instagram used square format images optimised for a smartphone screen. They were unencumbered by text, essays or other files. Photos and videos uploaded to the service can be edited with various filters to achieve stylistic effects. Recipients can 'tag', or add notes, to the posts, naming the location and the individuals who feature in the picture. More recently, the app has embraced 'stories', whereby users can post photos and videos in a sequential feed, with each post only accessible for 24 hours. Instagram is the epitome of fast media.

FUN FACT

INSTAGRAM CREATORS KEVIN SYSTROM AND MIKE KRIEGER SOLD THE APP TO FACEBOOK IN 2012 FOR $1 BILLION ONLY 18 MONTHS AFTER LAUNCH.

If you have an Instagram account, you'll see images from your friends, but you can easily look at posts from other users. The 'explore' feature and the use of hashtags – key words preceded by the hash symbol # – encourage users to sample various offerings. For example, users can select all Instagram posts with the same hashtag to see a range of images on the same topic. These will also lead you to subjects that might be trending, and these typically reach vast global audiences. The 'churn', or the speed with which a post trends (is viewed by exponentially large numbers of people) and then dies out, is amazingly fast.

While Instagram is the traditional home of food shots (these make up approximately 70% of all posts!), it's also widely used by celebrities (actress Selena Gomez and footballer Cristiano Ronaldo had the largest followings in 2018). Notably, it has also given rise to 'influencers' – often young and attractive females – who garner such huge numbers of followers that they are paid by advertisers to promote products. Thanks to the recent push for transparency online, influencers are now obliged to disclose what content they are being paid to promote.

'WE BELIEVE YOU CAN SEE THE WORLD HAPPENING IN REAL TIME THROUGH INSTAGRAM. AND I THINK THAT'S TRUE WHETHER IT'S TAYLOR SWIFT'S 1989 TOUR ... OR AN IMPORTANT MOMENT LIKE A PROTEST OVERSEAS, OR A MARCH LIKE "JE SUIS CHARLIE" IN PARIS.'

Kevin Systrom, co-founder of Instagram

Twitter

TWITTER came onto the market in 2006. It was all about text, but brevity was key: messages had to be 140 characters or less, with the idea of sharing off-the-cuff short thoughts. Millennials embraced it, and members of older generations also developed a fondness for composing and reading Twitter posts, or 'tweets'.

Part of Twitter's appeal was that people had started using Facebook poorly, and many users were tiring of the 'Facebook essay' – long, rambling, public opinion posts. Twitter, the polar opposite, gave an opportunity to post a brief, pithy, potentially comedic comment or response and move on. It was apparently too pithy, as the maximum tweet length was increased to 280 characters in November 2017.

'SORRY LOSERS AND HATERS, BUT MY I.Q. IS ONE OF THE HIGHEST – AND YOU ALL KNOW IT! PLEASE DON'T FEEL SO STUPID OR INSECURE, IT'S NOT YOUR FAULT.'

US President Donald Trump (via Twitter)

Like Instagram posts, tweets go out to anyone who happens to be following you. Tweets are used by many politicians, comedians and public figures to give their followers – who may number in the millions – a good idea of what they're thinking and doing.

If you have a Twitter account, you're not obligated to post anything: you can simply read the tweets posted by people you follow, which is known as 'lurking'.

Along with Instagram, Twitter is part of the fast-moving social media space. What matters in fast social media is what is 'trending' – the term for posts being read and liked, and/or shared ('retweeted') by many users in a short space of time. A trend starts if an individual enjoys a tweet so much or the news is so hot that they retweet it straightaway; if they have a lot of followers who respond similarly, a tweet can be read by hundreds of thousands of people all around the world within minutes. Another word for this a 'twitter storm'. When a message is passed on, liked and then retweeted, this creates a self-reinforcing cycle; the message spreads wider and wider until it burns out – probably because it is superseded by the next hot-off-the-press tweet. Hashtags also help this process along.

The speed of this form of social media means that Twitter has become the place of breaking news. Members of the general public who happen to be present as a story unfolds, such as the dramatic rescue of a group of young boys from a cave in Thailand, can sometimes tweet updates – in this case with the hashtag #caverescue – faster than many traditional news outlets, so Twitter has proved disruptive to journalism. Perhaps this is why it has been used so extensively by US President Donald Trump, who is wary of reporters and popularised the term 'fake news'.

Twitter can also play a pivotal role in social movements. Numerous riots and demonstrations have been organised through Twitter, thanks to the ease of connecting people who don't know each other directly. Think of #jesuischarlie and #metoo, both of which trended on Twitter.

Inevitably, something trending on Twitter will be picked up on Facebook, Instagram and Reddit and will generally appear across all social media platforms.

BEING 'TWITTERPATED' IS AN ACTUAL THING: IT'S 'WHEN YOU'RE OVERWHELMED WITH INFORMATION OR YOU'RE JUST SO EXCITED THAT YOU FORGET TO TWEET OR FORGET TO SHARE',

according to Jack Dorsey, CEO and co-founder of Twitter

Memes

I T was before the internet took off that scientist Richard Dawkins coined the term 'meme'. He broke new ground by comparing the evolution of ideas in human culture with the evolution of organisms. Just as the basic unit of organic evolution is the gene, he named the basic unit of replication of ideas the meme.

In biological terms, organisms like germs can replicate and evolve much more quickly if they are provided opportunities to spread to new organisms. But with the advent of the internet, the speed with which memes can cross vast distances quickly has outstripped their biological equivalent. Social media has led to the development of superbug memes, which are very good at getting people to share them, stopping them from dying out.

FUN FACT

THERE ARE 17,000 DIFFERENT CATEGORIES OF MEME ON THE 'KNOW YOUR MEME' DATABASE – A WEBSITE DEDICATED TO DOCUMENTING THIS INTERNET PHENOMENON.

Among the first superbug memes were chain emails and lolcats – cute cat pictures, usually accompanied by witty captions guaranteed to raise a smile. In modern terms, a meme often takes the form of a word or phrase superimposed on an image, a short video or a moving image called a 'GIF'. Another feature of memes is that they're liable to change; often people make their own versions of them. Some memes that have gone viral – in other words, were shared online millions of times – include 'planking', which involved posting a photo of someone lying down in a public place, and the 'Harlem Shake', which involved uploading a short video of people dancing to the song of the same name.

Memes have developed from individual internet in-jokes into a full visual language, used to communicate about every topic under the sun. They're used extensively on sites like Facebook, Reddit and the website 4chan, often combining multiple layers of meaning that aren't immediately apparent to oldies.

'AN INTERNET MEME IS A HIJACKING OF THE ORIGINAL IDEA. INSTEAD OF MUTATING BY RANDOM CHANCE AND SPREADING BY A FORM OF DARWINIAN SELECTION, INTERNET MEMES ARE ALTERED DELIBERATELY BY HUMAN CREATIVITY.'

Richard Dawkins

Reddit

WITH the development of the internet came myriad ways in which people could interact online. Some websites offered visitors the chance to subscribe (sign up) and become part of an online community united by a common purpose or issue. What started as a bulletin board – a site where information such as articles, news and events could be shared – was developed by students Alexis Ohanian, Steve Huffman and Aaron Schwartz into an out-of-the-box news site. They named their site Reddit, which is a play on 'read it'.

Reddit's point of difference is its approach to user participation. Content is user generated, plus the value and importance of posts on the site depends on how users vote on them. If something good or valuable is submitted, it will receive positive comments and be 'upvoted' by users. It will subsequently be made more readily available to others; that is, the link to the article will appear closer to the top of the feed. If it's bad, users can 'downvote' it, so it will become harder to locate – it may even

FUN FACT

REDDIT'S MASCOT, SNOO, STARTED AS A DOODLE BY CO-FOUNDER ALEXIS OHANIAN. SNOO IS GENDERLESS, HAS NO FINGERS, AND ITS LOOK CHANGES DEPENDING ON THE SUBREDDIT IN WHICH IT APPEARS.

disappear from the feed. Comments on posts are voted on in the same way: if a comment is highly visible, it means it's popular.

Reddit is structured with a front page and a number of 'subreddits' – individual feeds organised around specific subjects or themes, such as 'r/Funny', 'r/AskReddit', and 'r/UpliftingNews'. Anyone can make their own subreddit and moderate it themself – so there are pages for things as diverse as zombies, Marvel movies, auto detailing and crochet. The most popular articles from these subreddits make it to the front page.

You can also make your own customised subscription to reflect your interests so that your feed features popular content from whatever subreddits you choose.

Reddit has immense reach and influence among Millennials, with 330 million unique users per month as of 2019. It's the third-most-visited site in the United States and refers to itself as the 'frontpage of the internet'. Among its positive achievements are several impressive philanthropic charity efforts and hosting the world's largest Secret Santa – a carefully orchestrated gift exchange between strangers. However, the platform has also seen more than its fair share of drama. This includes the banning of controversial and radical subreddits, the hosting of online witch-hunts – such as accusing innocent people of participating in the Boston Marathon Bombing – and the widespread posting of leaked celebrity photos in 2014.

'FACEBOOK MAKES ME HATE THE PEOPLE I KNOW, AND REDDIT MAKES ME LOVE THE PEOPLE I DON'T.'

Alexis Ohanian, Reddit co-founder

Echo
Chambers

THE ECHO CHAMBER EFFECT IS COMMONLY CITED AS A GROWING FACTOR IN CONTEMPORARY POLITICS. SOME COMMENTATORS BELIEVE IT PLAYED A BIG PART IN THE SUCCESS OF DONALD TRUMP IN THE 2016 US PRESIDENTIAL ELECTION, AND THE RESULT OF THE UK BREXIT REFERENDUM THAT SAME YEAR.[1]

ONE of the downsides of social media – particularly your news feed – is that it's designed to present to you only topics you want to see. At face value, this may seem to be a good thing – saving you time, for instance – but it can have negative outcomes. When all that you see is largely influenced by what you already like, subscribe to or approve of, the filtering algorithms are inclined never to challenge you with anything new. This is the phenomenon of the 'filter bubble', in which you are only encouraged to engage with content you approve of, and anything that's converse to your views – including difficult subjects or opinions you might dislike – is filtered out of your awareness.

Viewed through that lens, a social media platform like Facebook can become an 'echo chamber', because when you log on, you will only interact with people who like the same things as you. As you can imagine, this can lead to narrow-mindedness, entrenched views and – in its darkest manifestation – reinforce antisocial beliefs or even encourage extremism. On a lighter note, for advertisers, it makes targeting advertisements a breeze.

Nevertheless, while feeds can influence your perceptions, there's nothing stopping you from tapping into the vast potential of the internet and choosing to engage with a broader spectrum of communities and opinions. The key to combating the echo chamber effect, whether on Facebook, Reddit or YouTube, is to consciously choose a balanced range of things to like or subscribe to, politically, socially and culturally. Another strategy is to get your news from outside social media, ideally from more than one source.

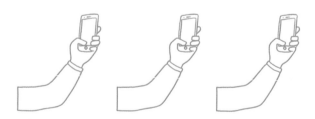

'[SOCIAL MEDIA] LETS YOU GO OFF WITH LIKE-MINDED PEOPLE, SO YOU'RE NOT MIXING AND SHARING AND UNDERSTANDING OTHER POINTS OF VIEW ... IT'S TURNED OUT TO BE MORE OF A PROBLEM THAN I, OR MANY OTHERS, WOULD HAVE EXPECTED.'

Bill Gates, principal founder of Microsoft Corporation

YouTube

WITH the development of online sites and connectivity, text and images became easy to share, but videos continued to cause problems due to their file size. YouTube was established in 2005 by three former employees of PayPal to remedy this issue, and it became a global success almost instantly.

YouTube allows users to upload, view and rate video content as well as comment on and subscribe to the content of other users. It hosts content ranging from user-generated original pieces to corporate media videos, short films, video blogging (or 'vlogging') and live streaming. While anyone can watch content on the platform, users have to be registered in order to upload and comment on content. Millennials are extensive viewers of short-form video online.

FUN FACT

IN FEBRUARY 2017, MORE THAN 400 HOURS OF CONTENT WERE BEING UPLOADED TO YOUTUBE EVERY MINUTE, AND OVER 1 BILLION HOURS OF CONTENT WERE BEING WATCHED EVERY DAY.

The value of YouTube was made clear when it was bought by Google in 2006 for US$1.65 billion. Google started putting ads at the beginning of the content, and YouTube was soon generating significant income. Google also introduced the practice where content creators are paid a sliding fee, depending on how many people actually watch the content, turning it into a platform where contributors can make serious money.

Many of the top YouTube stars – such as Swedish national Felix Kjellberg, who calls himself PewDiePie (it rhymes with cutie pie) – are young people who by regularly posting entertaining videos have gone on to build extraordinarily large followings and to amass fortunes.[1] Their natural presentation – without the overt image strategies of a professional set-up – allows viewers to feel that they are authentic and genuine, and to build a stronger connection with them. Subscribers find these grassroots personalities more relatable than traditional celebrities, and warm to the fact that they offer a subculture that *doesn't* appeal to older generations.

'WHEN I STARTED MY YOUTUBE CHANNEL IN 2010, I NEVER IMAGINED THAT ONE DAY IT WOULD BE THE MOST SUBSCRIBED CHANNEL IN THE WORLD AND THAT I WOULD BE A PART OF SUCH A GREAT COMMUNITY.'

PewDiePie, one of the top 10 YouTubers, with more than 80 million subscribers

Streaming

MOST people are avid consumers of entertainment, no matter which generation they belong to. Unlike previous generations, Millennials have grown up accessing multiple sources of entertainment on demand, wherever they happen to be, thanks to a technology called 'streaming'. This is the process by which a file can begin playing on a device before it has finished downloading from its originator.

The availability of streaming grew hand in hand with the growth of effective broadband and mobile networks. Once files could be downloaded at a speed greater than the time taken to listen to them or view them, streaming became practical and consumers rejoiced. Music was the first form of entertainment to be streamed because audio files are relatively small and easy to compress. As soon as streaming music became the norm, visits to record shops to buy music became a thing of the past – other than by the few aficionados who still valued the auditory clarity of vinyl.

FUN FACT

THE SUBSCRIPTION VIDEO ON DEMAND (SVOD) MARKET IN AUSTRALIA GREW BY 54% FROM JUNE 2017 TO JUNE 2018, WITH REVENUES GROWING UP TO 90% FOR THE SAME PERIOD.

Video was more problematic as file sizes were much larger. Before long, however, developments in available bandwidth and file-compression technology meant that providers could send high-definition video in real time – it could be watched as the next section loaded. This enabled the rise of the home-streaming industry, courtesy of companies like Netflix and Stan, which bypassed and soon eclipsed traditional media distribution channels: they replaced bricks-and-mortar rental companies like Blockbuster and took market share from cable providers like Time Warner, now WarnerMedia.

A cornerstone of consumers' enthusiastic uptake of streaming has been the availability of cheap data plans for smartphones. The ongoing demand for higher resolution continues to drive the increasing need for mobile bandwidth, reflected in offerings from various telecommunications companies ('telcos' for short).

Live streaming is also now commonplace. Many social media platforms enable users to stream their own videos of real events to the public as they happen.

MUSIC STREAMING

Most music streaming services charge a monthly subscription fee that allows access to pretty much every popular music track available in any mainstream genre – rock, jazz, disco or chart music.

Having access to one of these services has for the most part replaced buying music, except for when it's not available for streaming.

At the time of writing, the main service providers are:

- Spotify
- Apple Music
- Google Play Music/YouTube Red
- Pandora
- Tidal

MEDIA STREAMING

As with music streaming, media streaming services generally work on a subscription model, with a monthly fee granting you access to a wide range of movies, TV series, documentaries and other material.

Interestingly, once the new media streaming companies had mastered the distribution of these products, they disrupted the longstanding model of movie and TV studios by moving into the development and production of their own material. Many of the following service providers now create their own unique content, which they provide exclusively to their customers.

- Netflix
- Amazon Prime Video
- HBO
- Stan
- On-demand TV, eg in Australia ABC iview, SBS On Demand

OTHER STREAMING SERVICES

Social media platforms have also embraced streaming. YouTube led the way in this space, with the first worldwide online broadcast of a major sporting event in 2010 – cricket matches from the Indian Premier League – as well as a concert by U2 and a question-and-answer session with US President Barack Obama. Importantly, they also provide a vehicle for the streaming of content other than professionally produced media, ie content produced by their subscribers.

Video game streaming has also gained in popularity, with 33% of people subscribed to gaming services such as Xbox Live, Playstation Network and EA Access.[1] Sites like Twitch are also popular, streaming footage of individuals playing computer games and chatting about tactics. Again, these are supported by advertisers, but also by subscriptions from viewers.

Podcasts are a rapidly growing form of entertainment and engagement for Millennials, and are also freely accessible on the same devices that they use for music streaming. These are episodic series of digital audio files, which users download to listen to at the time of their choosing. As a natural replacement for radio and TV, podcasts are an increasingly popular way for Millennials to stay connected to their interests, with over 42% of 18–34 year olds listening to podcasts at least once a week.[2]

The attraction of podcasts is that they're easy and efficient, and fulfil the on-demand mentality common to Millenials. While podcasts from media personalities make for popular entertainment, they are also the perfect delivery vehicle for non-fiction and reality content. The ability to access deeper dives into events and issues allows users to seek out information on any subject that appeals to them.

'IT TURNS OUT THAT ALL NETFLIX STREAMING PEAK ON SATURDAY NIGHT CAN FIT INSIDE A SINGLE FIBER OPTIC, WHICH IS THE SIZE OF ONE HUMAN HAIR.'

Reed Hastings, Netflix CEO

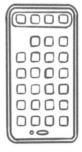
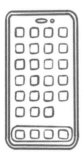
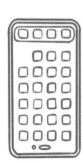

The Cloud

INITIALLY, the concept for the internet was that each user would have a small computer, or terminal, linked to a larger mainframe computer. The mainframe would do the bulk of any processing or calculations and send the results back to that terminal. Gradually, however, as computers became cheaper and more powerful, there was a move away from centralised computing and towards the personal computer, or 'PC'.

'CLOUD IS ABOUT HOW YOU DO COMPUTING, NOT WHERE YOU DO COMPUTING.'
Paul Maritz, CEO of VMWare

When the World Wide Web took off, hosting all the websites and responding to the interactions with those websites made things more complicated. The further development of the responsive web, with features such as drop-down boxes and the introduction of shopping carts to facilitate e-commerce, meant that servers – programs or devices that provide functionality for other programs or devices in a network – had to become more and more sophisticated. Eventually, servers ended up basically replacing mainframes and doing the majority of the processing required.

Recently, we have seen the renaissance of the mainframe as part of the mix, and when people talk about 'the Cloud' or 'Cloud computing', they're talking about functions that occur on these ultra-powerful machines. Using the advanced connectivity of the internet, today's PC users can access not one, but many different mainframes. The work of producing the responsive web is done in the abstract Cloud, which hides all the work of interfacing data centres and servers to make the service appear seamless. This gives instant connection to shared pools of resources and services, without users having to worry where the data or computation is hosted.

Millennials are highly familiar with Cloud providers – companies offering this service – the biggest of which are Google Cloud, Amazon's AWS and Apple's iCloud. These companies spread the data that they store around the world, so that it's accessible from anywhere, and specialise in getting information in and out of their centres quickly and efficiently. While smaller companies might build their own data centres and manage their own Clouds, often they will also rent space or capacity from the big players.

ONE OF THE ISSUES WITH MAINFRAMES IS THAT THEY HEAT UP. THIS EXPLAINS WHY THE WORLD'S LARGEST DATA CENTRE IS LOCATED IN THE REMOTE NORTH OF THE ARCTIC CIRCLE, WHERE THE COLD CLIMATE AND ACCESS TO HYDRO POWER HELP TRIM POWER COSTS BY 60%.

The Internet of Things

THANKS to advances in the development of devices using electronics and software, coupled with the development and availability of the internet, there are now devices that can connect with each other, interact, exchange data and be remotely controlled. This is known as the Internet of Things (IoT), and is a growing and accepted part of the Millennials' world.

Examples of IoT in everyday life are home appliances such as fridges, washing machines and even mattresses that can be programmed to be cost efficient, productive and responsive. New fridges can sense that there's no milk left and put in an automatic order to a retailer. Washing machines can use sensors to decide on the weight and fabrics and select the relevant cycle. Mattresses can adjust the tension of the springs, detect when you roll over, monitor your sleep cycles and manage heating settings to give you the optimum conditions for restorative sleep. There's no limit to where this can end.

Not all applications of this technology are domestic. There are systems that can monitor for medical emergencies, check blood pressure and send back information to health professionals on the working of heart monitors and pacemakers – sometimes over large distances. In transport, interaction between all parts of a system allows smart and rapid responses to monitoring, which enables efficient traffic control and the management and reporting of public transport options. In manufacturing, intelligent systems can program dynamic responses to product demands and the optimisation of production.

THERE HAS BEEN EXPLOSIVE GROWTH IN THE RANGE AND NUMBER OF DEVICES CONNECTED AND CONTROLLED BY THE INTERNET. WE ARE ADDING ABOUT 100 THINGS TO THE INTERNET EVERY SECOND, AND IT'S ESTIMATED THAT THERE WILL BE 30 BILLION DEVICES CONNECTED BY 2020.

There are some downsides to the gathering of data from disparate devices. The trade-off for the convenience of these appliances is a compromise of privacy: while the information collected is a valuable tool for manufacturers in their development of products, the data can be easily sold on to others. There's also a second trade-off: if a cheap computer is used to make something work, its cyber security is almost definitely non-existent. There may be danger in someone exploiting those security loopholes and making smart appliances act smarter than you would like.

'AS THE INTERNET OF THINGS ADVANCES, THE VERY NOTION OF A CLEAR DIVIDING LINE BETWEEN REALITY AND VIRTUAL REALITY BECOMES BLURRED, SOMETIMES IN CREATIVE WAYS.'

Geoff Mulgan, PhD, social innovation commentator

Smart
Homes

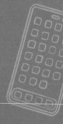

I N the 1960s, the futuristic life portrayed by animated TV program The Jetsons existed only in our imaginations, the comic's labour-saving devices seen as impossibilities. No longer! Once cheaper and more powerful computers were developed, coupled with the reach of the internet, smart appliances were born. With the Internet of Things now a reality, the day could soon come when smart appliances will not only order your milk, wash your clothes efficiently or give you a good night's sleep, but a voice-activated interface linked to a Cloud service could take control of your whole house.

Already, there are virtual personal assistants such as Alexa (Amazon), Siri (Apple) or the Google Assistant, that will listen to your requests and carry them out, whether it's to draft an email and send it or play a specific song on Spotify. The next obvious development is for a provider like Amazon or

FUN FACT

THE TECHNOLOGY ALREADY EXISTS FOR SMART LIGHTING TO BE CONTROLLED FROM YOUR PHONE. THE BRIGHTNESS, COLOUR OF THE LIGHTS OR WHETHER THEY ARE ON OR OFF CAN ALL BE MANAGED WITH A FEW TAPS – AND NEW LED LIGHTS DON'T BURN OUT!

Google to take over an entire house, coordinating all the smart appliances and connecting directly to them all. Through microphones, home owners could simply speak to control all the appliances in the house.

Unfortunately, a high level of reliance on this technology would expose home owners to potential cybersecurity weaknesses. Should those possibilities be realised, the health, safety and security consequences could be serious. It would also leave home owners vulnerable to extensive breaches of privacy or manipulation. Once data from every aspect of the household can be gathered, collated and assessed by a single company – one that may well be interested in feeding you advertising or ordering and providing whatever you need for same-day delivery – you could find yourself completely locked in.

'THERE WILL BE ALL KINDS OF HICCUPS, HORROR STORIES, ACCIDENTS, DELIBERATE ACTS OF SABOTAGE AND OTHER BUMPS ALONG THE ROAD THAT WILL SLOW BUT NOT STOP OUR GREATER CONNECTIVITY. CONVENIENCE AND EMPOWERMENT ALWAYS SEEM TO WIN FOR MOST PEOPLE, EVEN AT SOME LOSS OF PRIVACY, CONTROL OR TRANSPARENCY.'

Scott McLeod, US educator and technology commentator

(Lack of) Online Privacy

IN society generally, it has long been believed that everyone has an entitlement to privacy. In fact, this fundamental human right is enshrined in the UN Declaration of Human Rights.[1]

As people became accustomed to communicating online, they brought with them the assumption that privacy problems would only emerge if an individual had direct communication with someone else whose security was compromised or who was unethical. For tech-savvy Millennials, however, electronic privacy is regarded as something that genuinely doesn't exist. If you want to live and work in a modern technological world, almost nothing you do is, or can be, private.

'RELYING ON THE GOVERNMENT TO PROTECT YOUR PRIVACY IS LIKE ASKING A PEEPING TOM TO INSTALL YOUR WINDOW BLINDS.'

John Perry Barlow, internet civil liberties advocate

It is now widely known that platforms like Facebook and Google have access to enormous amounts of data about you, including your location, spending habits, and your browsing history. Conversely, since the advent of smartphones and fast social media like Twitter and Instagram, you're pushed towards broadcasting everything you do.

If you wish to safeguard your online privacy and are prepared to put in the effort required, there are measures available. DuckDuckGo, for instance, markets itself as 'the search engine that doesn't track you'.[2] Jaded Millennials would advise you to save yourself the effort, that defending your privacy is already a lost battle and – as far as going online is concerned – to feel the fear and do it anyway.

FUN FACT

ASSUME THAT PRETTY MUCH EVERY COMPANY YOU INTERACT WITH ONLINE WILL STORE EVERY SKERRICK OF INFORMATION DOWN TO THE CLICK LEVEL AND WILL SELL IT ON. SADLY, THE LESS SCRUPULOUS ONLINE OPERATORS MAY STEAL THAT DATA IN ORDER TO SELL IT.

Because technology moves fast, legislators have to constantly play catch-up when it comes to protecting the interests of individuals online. In some jurisdictions, like Australia, regulations exist to prevent companies exploiting information they gather. So, for example, insurance companies who access information about individuals from genetic testing laboratories are unable to charge them more for products on the basis of perceived risk factors. They can, however, discuss preventative measures – based on the same information – so that those clients won't become a liability to them long-term.

One organisation trying to exert influence in this sphere is the Electronic Frontiers Foundation (EFF).[3] It monitors policy developments and advocates, among other things, that all software should be free. The EFF fights against the insidious failure to protect the privacy of individuals, and they are known for taking donations, hiring good lawyers and suing companies who use information poorly or illegally.

Google

THE next of the three internet giants is Google. Originally, it was purely a search engine, offering internet users an efficient way to discover content on the web. While there were many search engines offering this service, the difference and strength of Google was its clever algorithms, which ranked the websites that it directed users to. The 'PageRank' algorithm – a term that incorporated the name of Google co-founder Larry Page – ranked a particular page depending on the number of other reputable sites that linked to it. Users flocked to the new, faster search engine, and a new verb came into use: to 'google', or look something up.

Then Google realised that in order to turn a healthy profit, it would need to embrace advertising. Suddenly, when accessing web pages, Google users discovered that they were exposed to associated ads. The company also diversified into displaying

FUN FACT

WHEN GOOGLE INVENTED CHROME, MICROSOFT'S INTERNET EXPLORER HAD ALMOST 70% OF THE MARKET. IN JUST NINE YEARS, CHROME HELD OVER 60% OF THE MARKET AND NO OTHER PROVIDER HAD MORE THAN 10% MARKET SHARE.

ads on other people's websites, paying them for the space and serving the ads.

Google is an industry leader in many areas of technology. For example, the company saw that the available internet browsers were inefficient and were impacting its core business, so it developed its own – Chrome. Today, Chrome is the most used browser in the world. Google also provides a number of services that are ostensibly free: think Google Drive, Gmail, Google Translate, Google Maps, Google Earth, Google Calendar, Google Hangouts, Google Photos, and so on. By pulling people into their realm, Google can collate information on them for the purpose of offering highly targeted advertising, which in turn nets the company even more income.

In addition to its massive advertising revenue, Google has a diverse array of other income sources: some would say the company has its fingers in a lot of pies. For instance, it has moved into artificial intelligence (AI) research. Users of the Google Assistant can have full conversations and it will carry out tasks such as booking hair appointments or restaurants. The company also offers phone access without a sim card – it operates over the internet – and has invested development and research funds into areas as diverse as driverless cars, quantum computers and stratospheric balloons.

'WE WANT TO BUILD TECHNOLOGY THAT EVERYBODY LOVES USING, AND THAT AFFECTS EVERYONE. WE WANT TO CREATE BEAUTIFUL, INTUITIVE SERVICES AND TECHNOLOGIES THAT ARE SO INCREDIBLY USEFUL THAT PEOPLE USE THEM TWICE A DAY. LIKE THEY USE A TOOTHBRUSH. THERE AREN'T THAT MANY THINGS PEOPLE USE TWICE A DAY.'

Larry Page, co-founder of Google

Big
Data

SINCE the widespread adoption of the internet, companies have been able to access an insane amount of data. Traditionally, a business could gather data about what they bought and sold and the money made from carrying out their enterprise, and it was all relatively easy to store and analyse. In addition to that, contemporary businesses have the ability to track information as diverse as how customers come to their website, exactly what they look at, how long they look at it, the items that they click on, what their friends are buying and what reviews they're reading. It's a huge amount of information to analyse. Collectively, it's referred to, somewhat laconically, as 'Big Data'.

'WITHOUT BIG DATA ANALYTICS, COMPANIES ARE BLIND AND DEAF, WANDERING OUT ONTO THE WEB LIKE DEER ON A FREEWAY.'

Geoffrey Moore, prominent technology adoption consultant

Initially, digitally savvy businesses were focused on the volume, variety and velocity of their data, but as analytics improved, the veracity and value of that data also became more important.

These days, data is so plentiful and detailed that the emphasis is on 'mining' it, or making sense of it. In fact, the term Big Data has come to refer less to the actual information and more to the use of predictive analytics and other methods to extract the value and insights. This can uncover new correlations that can be useful to a business in making operational decisions, determining how they can benefit from the data – such as what ads to show people, and what offers to make to specific customers.

In a wider sense, data can be a scientific resource, so that industries such as healthcare can spot health trends more easily. To this end, career opportunities now exist in the area of data analytics, and many companies and organisations now employ data scientists or contract the services of data analytics companies and task them with finding insights that can be of benefit.

The sheer volume of the data that can be marshalled for analysis has had some interesting knock-on effects: businesses and organisations have had to buy web power to access supercomputers. This has further fuelled the rise of the big Cloud-computing companies such as Google, Amazon and Microsoft.

NOT ALL DATA ANALYTICS COMPANIES ARE COMMERCIAL IN FOCUS. SOME, SUCH AS PRIVATE CALIFORNIA-BASED FIRM PALANTIR TECHNOLOGIES, USE DATA FOR THE PURPOSES OF COUNTERTERRORISM ANALYSIS, FRAUD INVESTIGATIONS AND CYBERSECURITY. CIVIL RIGHTS ORGANISATIONS WARN THAT THERE CAN BE LARGE-SCALE PRIVACY IMPLICATIONS TO THESE STUDIES.

Amazon

THE third internet giant is Amazon. Founded by Jeff Bezos in 1994, it was originally an online bookshop that went up against the traditional retailers in the USA. By selling online, Amazon avoided the expenses of stocking and distribution and was able to pass the savings on to customers. They also achieved efficient delivery to customers, who responded enthusiastically to the ease with which they could obtain cheap reading material. This business model transformed the book retail market, and in March 2014, a stunning 65% of all titles sold online – print and e-books – were coming from Amazon.[1]

It was a natural progression for Amazon to expand their product range. A wide variety of new companies started to sell directly to consumers who had an Amazon account, taking advantage of Amazon's established distribution network. The company's logo emphasises that Amazon customers can go online and buy anything from A to Z. By 2005, they introduced Amazon Prime in the USA – a membership service with a small annual fee that offered two-day free shipping on anything Amazon sold.

FUN FACT

AMAZON ONCE WENT DOWN FOR 49 MINUTES, AND AS A DIRECT CONSEQUENCE THE COMPANY MISSED NEARLY US$5.7 MILLION IN SALES.

Like Google, Amazon likes to keep their customers within their own environment – by analysing customers' personal preferences then cross-selling them goods accordingly. Another strategy is to develop Amazon-brand offerings. Examples include Amazon Web Services (AWS), a Cloud computing service that has captured about 60% of the market; the Kindle e-book reader; and even Amazon-published books. The company has also branched into music (Amazon Music) and live streaming (Twitch). They've bought the Wholefoods supermarket chain in the USA, Canada and the UK. At the time of writing, Amazon are setting up cashierless grocery stores, where cameras follow you around the store and automatically bill you for whatever you place in your shopping bag.

Amazon's dominance of the retail market has radically changed the landscape and made life hard for other retailers – many of which have had to adapt and offer their own products through Amazon's platform.

'I DON'T THINK [AMAZON.COM] WANTS TO OWN A PIECE OF RETAIL, THEY WANT TO OWN ALL OF IT.'

Scott Galloway, academic and commentator on the digital economy

Online Shopping

As soon as the internet was operational, it opened the way for online shopping. Initially, payment was tricky, and offerings were limited to low-cost items that had worked well through mail order or over the phone, such as music, wine, flowers and chocolate.

Things really took off in the early 1990s with the invention of modern internet cryptography, which enabled secure credit card transactions. The first secure online purchase recorded was a pizza from Pizza Hut in 1994. The following year, budding ecommerce giants eBay – the first big platform for online shopping open to retailers and individuals – and Amazon – at that stage purely an online bookshop – adopted the secure transaction technology, and consumers began overcoming their reticence. The barrier to spending online dropped further in 1998 with the debut of PayPal, a revolutionary system that enabled arms-length financial transactions. After setting up an account with this worldwide online payment system, consumers could make online purchases on PayPal-friendly websites without having to key in their bank or credit details.

Online shopping is the norm for the Millennial generation. They research items online, accessing comparison sites to identify particular features of products – often without reference to either a manufacturer's usually biased website or a physical store. Accessing reviews also contributes to a purchase decision, after which it's easy to find where the item can be purchased at the best price or most convevient location.

The main advantage of online shopping is convenience – it's possible shop at all hours of the night and day, from a train, from home in your pyjamas, from remote areas. Retailers typically offer speedy delivery, low prices, and free returns on basically any item, coupled with social media strategies and targeted online advertising.

Online shopping has been the perfect vehicle for newly developed digital services, for which there are no physical objects changing hands. Retailers can ship computer software, music, video and e-books electronically with ease.

There are still some commodities that are not suitable for online shopping. Generally, the more expensive the item, the more traditional the buying process – especially with goods where the purchasing is part of the experience, like luxury cars or jewellery. Items where you need to test the quality, feel or fit, such as a new guitar or custom-made clothing, are also best purchased in person.

'WE SEE OUR CUSTOMERS AS INVITED GUESTS TO A PARTY, AND WE ARE THE HOSTS. IT'S OUR JOB EVERY DAY TO MAKE EVERY IMPORTANT ASPECT OF THE CUSTOMER EXPERIENCE A LITTLE BIT BETTER.'

Jeff Bezos, Amazon founder and CEO

Fashion

LIKE every generation before them, Millennials have their own distinctive take on fashion. If anything, their style can be characterised as about breaking all the rules, wanting to pull together their own identity and refusing to be pigeonholed. This might mean mixing masculine and feminine elements, and favouring versatile pieces that move easily between an office environment and a social occasion.

The move towards experimentation and the merging of different styles has led to the rise of innovative designers, and high-energy trendy retailers are taking over from the old reliables offering the same staples in the high street. Conforming to styles or trends dictated by traditional retailers on a seasonal basis makes no sense to this generation.

In general, Millennials go for a more casual and comfortable aesthetic, with business casual now the default in most office settings and exercise wear moving more into the fashion space. In fact, some old-school brands, like Levi's, are experiencing a rise in sales thanks to this more relaxed standard in workplace attire.

Online businesses, such as The Iconic and ASOS, have fine-tuned their production and delivery systems to promote spending and push trends through at a rapid rate, which is where the term 'fast fashion' comes from. Their success is largely attributable to their canny social media strategies and ability to understand and maintain relationships with their target audiences. Social media is also used extensively to feature brands favoured by influencers such as Kendall Jenner and Gigi Hadid.

For online retailers, or 'e-tailers', fast fashion and online shopping are a match made in heaven. However, as Millennials become more aware of the wider impacts of this behaviour, they're questioning it. Social commentators are noting the emergence of the 'slow fashion' movement, which encourages minimisation of an organisation's carbon footprint, high standards for workers' rights and the use of environmentally sustainable materials. There are also strong trends towards shopping in second-hand stores, swapping with friends and returning used clothes to be recycled in exchange for discounts. These practices reflect Millennials' concern for the world in general.

'IT ISN'T ENOUGH JUST LOOKING FOR QUALITY IN THE PRODUCTS WE BUY, WE MUST ENSURE THAT THERE IS QUALITY IN THE LIVES OF THE PEOPLE WHO MAKE THEM.'

Orsola de Castro, designer of ethical fashion

Bitcoin and Blockchain

NEW technology has facilitated changes to conventional thinking in many fields, but equally, technology can arise in response to ideas. For instance, re-envisioning the concept of centralised banking and governments' control over the supply of money prompted the idea for the online decentralised financial system with its own currency, known as Bitcoin. Think of it like this: if the internet were a country, bitcoin would be its currency.

An individual called Satoshi Nakamoto, whose true identity is unknown, is credited with devising the technology for Bitcoin. Essentially, he created a peer-to-peer version of electronic cash that allows online payments to be sent directly from one party to another without going through a financial institution, and it's serviced entirely by the internet. The Bitcoin network is not run by a single person or company. According to a 2017 *New York Times* article, as of October 2017, about 9500 computers all around the world helped maintain the network, and the records of the Bitcoin

FUN FACT

BITCOIN FANS CELEBRATE 22 MAY, OR BITCOIN PIZZA DAY. ON THIS DAY IN 2010, BITCOIN WAS FIRST USED – TO BUY TWO PAPA JOHN'S PIZZAS FOR 10,000 BITCOINS!

network, including all balances and transactions ever undertaken, are stored on every one of those computers.[1] Each transaction is validated and relayed to all the other users once there is a new block of valid transactions. This record – effectively a ledger – is called a 'blockchain'.

Controversially, however, Bitcoin operates with anonymity. The ledger keeps track of accounts called 'wallets': coins moving between wallets are tracked on the blockchain, but the ownership of any given wallet is a secret.

Adding these blocks of transactions to the blockchain is known as 'mining' bitcoin. The right to add these blocks goes to whoever wins a complex guessing game; to be added to the blockchain, each block must be accompanied by a special number that depends on the block's contents. Bitcoin was designed so that the best way to find the right number to add is by just guessing it, and the first person to guess the right number can add the block to the chain, and receive a prize of new bitcoins for their troubles. New bitcoin blocks are mined on average every 10 minutes.

For many, the attraction of Bitcoin is that there is no government involvement, the transactions are not reported and are completely private. Instead of a government or institution backing the currency, it's backed by maths and cryptography. Unsurprisingly, however, bitcoin has been used in illegal transactions. Among other criticisms are its high electricity consumption and price volatility. Despite these issues, decentralised currency is a part of the future.

'BITCOIN IS BETTER THAN CURRENCY IN THAT YOU DON'T HAVE TO BE PHYSICALLY IN THE SAME PLACE AND, OF COURSE, FOR LARGE TRANSACTIONS, CURRENCY CAN GET PRETTY INCONVENIENT.'

Bill Gates, principal founder of Microsoft Corporation

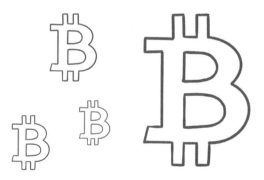

LinkedIn

IN 2003 – before the social media apps that now dominate the life of Millennials were established – a business app named LinkedIn, which connected people socially, made its first appearance on the internet. Reid Hoffman, an early internet entrepreneur, recognised that people liked building and leveraging networks in the business world, and believed it would be valuable to exploit those connections. He was proved right – the site had a million users within two years and now boasts a membership of over half a billion people.

FUN FACT

LINKEDIN HAS ACTIVE PROFILES IN OVER 200 COUNTRIES, INCLUDING CHINA, WHERE FACEBOOK AND TWITTER ARE BANNED.

LinkedIn is a social network designed to connect business and career professionals, and for people to build strategic relationships. You start by creating a professional profile – which generally includes the basics of your resumé, a summary of your skills, contact information and any other relevant information. You then connect to others. The idea is to create as many connections as you can by adding people in your own professional circle and then widening your network to include their connections. These connections can endorse your skills as well as allow you to access resources, find work or clients, and build alliances and partnerships.

One of LinkedIn's main functions is to facilitate the recruitment process, allowing recruiters to search for potential candidates as well as allowing those candidates to access information on people who are hiring, and to explore any mutual connections.

Companies – as well as individuals – can cultivate an active presence on LinkedIn by publishing articles and resources. This may challenge traditional journalism in the business sphere.

Joining LinkedIn at a basic level is free, but most of the company's income now comes from paid subscriptions. These offer enhanced functionality, such as allowing subscribers to connect with people they don't know directly, facilitating valuable connections for recruiters and sales professionals. Another income stream is from advertising, although it is less intrusive and more targeted than on other social media sites – helping LinkedIn to be widely considered as a reputable business site.

'ONE OF THE GREAT THINGS ABOUT LINKEDIN IS IT ISN'T THE SAME KIND OF NETWORKING THAT HAPPENS AT CONVENTIONS, WHERE YOU'RE WEARING A NAME TAG, TRYING TO MEET STRANGERS, AND AWKWARDLY ATTEMPTING TO MAKE SMALL TALK. LINKEDIN IS NETWORKING WITHOUT THE PRESSURE.'

Melanie Pinola, author of
LinkedIn in 30 Minutes

Self-brand

WHEN it comes to purchasing goods and services, the power of a strong brand is obvious to all of us, but Millennials have come to recognise in equal measure the value of a personal and individual brand, in order to present and promote themselves. And they are invested in culturing, curating and protecting that brand.

The term was first used and discussed in a 1997 article by respected US business writer Tom Peters, and expanded upon by marketers David McNally and Karl Speak in their book *Be Your Own Brand* in which they define the concept this way: 'Your brand is a perception or emotion ... that describes the total experience of having a relationship with you.' Thanks to social media, this concept has been hypercharged.

Establishing a personal brand is seen as crucial for many Millennials in giving them control of how people see them, ensuring they can manage their reputation for greater success and career progression. To be effective, these brands need to be 'authentic, visible and consistent'.[1]

Social media is an integral part of establishing that brand, with individuals being able to more quickly gain visibility for things they are passionate about or good at. But while it's an efficient way to reach a wide range of people and network efficiently, an ill-timed tweet or inappropriate post can damage not only a personal reputation but a professional one.

Fresh opportunities have arisen for people to make a splash and cultivate their brand. One of the easiest is the blog (a contraction of the words 'web' and 'log'), an online diary hosted on a domain site. Essentially, anyone can publish their thoughts. The more successful among these bloggers, for instance the most popular of the 'mummy bloggers', can have so many followers that they receive invitations to appear on TV panels and even attract book deals.

A PERSONAL BRAND IS AN EXPECTATION OF THE EXPERIENCE PEOPLE WILL HAVE WITH YOU – IT GIVES YOU THE ABILITY TO STAND OUT FROM THE COMPETITION IN A WAY YOU DESIGN.

So assiduously do some Millennials build their brand – and establish those large numbers of online followers – that marketers deem them to be 'influencers'. At the extreme, influencers such as Kim Kardashian create such a strong brand image that they are called upon to endorse products – such is the power they personally wield in the media and the marketplace.

'BRANDING IS WHAT PEOPLE SAY ABOUT
YOU WHEN YOU ARE NOT IN THE ROOM.'

Jeff Bezos, Amazon founder and CEO

WhatsApp

COMMUNICATION has been revolutionised by the internet. As soon as phones became mobile, traditional, or 'landline', phones started to lose ground to them. With every successive innovation on the smartphone, such as paid SMS messaging, or 'texting', smartphones have become more versatile, and Millennials switch seamlessly between different modes of communication, each of which incorporates various combinations of voice, graphics, photos and video. Currently, web-based messaging apps are dominating. Millennials revel in these apps, which essentially allow free communication and are incredibly efficient in linking individuals or groups.

While originally these technologies were developed and deployed on personal computers (PCs) – MSN messenger and AOL messenger are two notable examples – once they were adapted for smartphones, they started gaining in popularity. One factor was the addition of push notifications, whereby an app will generate a message, eg to notify you that someone has messaged you, without you actually opening the app.

In 2009, the release of WhatsApp furthered the demise of the landline: the WhatsApp message travelled over the internet rather than the phone network. Although a phone number was required to sign up, where an internet connection existed, messaging was free. Since then, online messaging has grown to subsume the role of phone calls and text messages.

WhatsApp had set the bar for smartphone messaging technology and, as is inevitable with any innovation in this lucrative market, other companies raced to emulate its success, and devise even cleverer solutions. Facebook quickly released a mobile app called Facebook Messenger. Like WhatsApp, it allowed direct communication using the internet, but as it worked through Facebook profiles – following the precedent set by its computer-based messaging app, Facebook chat – it didn't require a phone number.

FUN FACT

ACCORDING TO RESEARCH BY SYDNEY-BASED AGENCY THE WORKS, 38% OF MESSAGING APP USERS REGARD THOSE APPS AS THEIR PRIMARY COMMUNICATION DEVICE, WITH EMAILS, VOICE CALLS AND TRADITIONAL SOCIAL MEDIA ALL SEEING SIGNIFICANT DECREASES.

The other main player in the smartphone market, Apple, put out iMessage. The messages show up as different colours, depending on which network they are using – green for internet, blue for cellular.

The domino effect set off by WhatsApp didn't stop there. As these widely adopted messaging apps rendered data more useful and text less dominant, telcos were forced to tweak their phone plans: many now offer free texts. In the future, the cellular network's relevance will entirely be that it provides data connectivity to the internet, with phone calls and text messages over the phone network becoming a thing of the past.

'WHATSAPP BEGAN AS A SIMPLE IDEA: ENSURING THAT ANYONE COULD STAY IN TOUCH WITH FAMILY AND FRIENDS ANYWHERE ON THE PLANET, WITHOUT COSTS OR GIMMICKS STANDING IN THE WAY.'

Jan Koum, co-founder of WhatsApp

Tinder

SINCE its inception, the web has had the potential to facilitate close personal connections, as evidenced by the proliferation of romance sections on bulletin boards. Then smartphones incorporated geolocation features: the capability of identifying the geographical location of a device and therefore the whereabouts of the person carrying that device by means of digital information processed via the internet.

Suddenly, apps on phones could make it easy to meet up with people in a specific location. It wasn't necessary to know the area or even the individual; your smartphone could guide you. Apps were built to cater for different tastes and situations: some people were looking for long-term involvement; others were interested in short-term physical encounters, or 'hookups'.

FUN FACT

TINDER IS AVAILABLE IN OVER 196 COUNTRIES AND IN 40 LANGUAGES. TO FACILITATE BETTER MATCHES, IT GIVES YOU A SECRET INTERNAL RATING, DEPENDING ON HOW DESIRABLE YOU ARE ON THE APP TO OTHERS!

Tinder, established in 2012, is the most prominent of a regime of relationship apps. It allows users to select potential partners directly from their phone then meet up, possibly even within minutes. By 2014 it had introduced to a new generation of daters the concept of 'swiping' – a way of quickly scanning through profiles and choosing a potential partner – and quickly amassed more than a billion swipes per day (with ads, of course, to make it a viable business model).

On Tinder, the profile is your starting point. This is where you upload a selection of photos of you and a biography that can be as creative as you choose. There is a caveat: so strict are the requirements of the app that it's very hard to fake basic information, such as your name and birthdate. When you actively seek an encounter, the site displays a series of prospective matches that are located near you. One by one, you view each person's profile and if you like what you see, you simply swipe right. If not, you swipe left. If two people swipe right on each other's profile, also known as 'matching', Tinder then lets them communicate directly through messaging.

The safety lies in the fact that at this stage they haven't swapped important information, like phone numbers or email addresses, yet can communicate without risk. Based on how this messaging goes – and aided by the biographical text in the profile – users then decide whether to arrange to meet in person.

Although Tinder is rife with 'openers' that signal users are seeking a casual arrangement, many people who meet on Tinder have formed conventional relationships.

Alternatives to Tinder include Grindr, set up for male-to-male connections, which tends to work explicitly for hookups. Then there are apps such as Bumble, which place more emphasis on fostering relationships. This app tries to give more power to women – only women can send the first message.

Dating apps have spawned new terminology:

GHOSTING: ending a personal relationship by suddenly, and without explanation, withdrawing from all communication.

CATFISHING: luring someone into a relationship by means of a fictional online persona.

> 'THESE COMPANIES DON'T CLAIM THAT THEY'RE GOING TO GIVE YOU YOUR SOULMATE, AND THEY DON'T CLAIM THAT YOU CAN TELL WHO'S COMPATIBLE WITH YOU FROM A PROFILE. YOU SIMPLY SWIPE ON THIS STUFF AND THEN MEET OVER A PINT OF BEER OR A CUP OF COFFEE.'
>
> *Eli Finkel, Social Psychology professor*

'It's Complicated' Relationships

THERE'S a field on your Facebook profile where you can disclose your relationship status, should you wish to. Among the available options – single, engaged, married, divorced, widowed and so on – is 'It's complicated'. This seems to epitomise the situation that many Millennials find themselves in when it comes to matters of the heart.

More and more Millennials are openly questioning their sexuality and/or identifying as non-heterosexual, and acceptance and understanding of these different statuses is growing. Between 1996 and 2016, the number of those identifying as being in same-sex partnerships more than quadrupled.[1]

FUN FACT

MILLENNIALS CAN EXPECT AN AVERAGE OF JUST 8 SEXUAL PARTNERS IN THEIR ADULTHOOD, DOWN FROM THE 11 OF THE BABY BOOMERS AND THE 10 OF GEN X.

Relative to earlier generations, Millennials are more likely to prioritise personal development, education, careers or obtaining financial stability ahead of being in a committed relationship, and it's not unusual for Millennials to class themselves as single. In the USA, the percentage of young adults who report not being married or in a committed relationship rose from 52% in 2004 to 64% in 2014.[2]

Many members of this generation saw their parents' relationship end in divorce. Consequently, living in monogamy may not be their expectation – though marriage is still seen by many as a potential endgame. The failure of conventional relationships, coupled with more widespread sexual liberation, has led to more open attitudes. Fairly relaxed arrangements are common, for instance an ambiguous state – between being friends and being in a committed relationship – sometimes referred to as 'friends with benefits'. Here, sex is casual, and other relationships or dating may not be ruled out.

It's typical for Millennials to work out the terms of their relationship and what is acceptable to them between themselves – and that applies no matter what the sexual orientation of the partners.

'THE SHEER AMOUNT OF CHOICE PRESENT IN TODAY'S DATING SCENE CAN MAKE COMMITMENT EVEN HARDER FOR A GENERATION WHO HAS BEEN CONDITIONED TO HAVE IT ALL.'

Tara Griffith Baker, US psychotherapist and relationship coach

The Rainbow – LGBTQIA+

UNLIKE most things Millennial, the LGBTQIA+ community actually has its roots way back in the 1960s. The sexual revolution led to more freedom and a move away from the strict gender roles and classifications that had previously existed. This brought various subcultures to the fore, and as there was no non-derogatory way to classify someone who wasn't heterosexual, the need for new labels arose.

'OPENNESS MAY NOT COMPLETELY DISARM PREJUDICE, BUT IT'S A GOOD PLACE TO START.'

Jason Collins, USA's first openly gay professional basketballer

Initially, there was a lot of in-fighting between these marginalised subcultural groups over appropriate labelling. In 1988, the acronym LGBT became acknowledged in the USA as representing lesbian, gay, bisexual and transgender individuals. Gradually, the acronym expanded to include Q (queer, or questioning, representing those who didn't feel they were explicitly included in the four original classifications), I (intersex – individuals born with sex characteristics that don't fit conventional male or female bodies), and A (asexual – people who are non-sexual). Other sexual orientations emerged, and can be indicated by the + sign, so that the acronym is inclusive of all sexual orientations. It's also commonly known as the 'alphabet soup'.

Back in June 1969, the Stonewall Riots in New York were spontaneous violent demonstrations by the LGBT community against police raids targeting homosexuals in Greenwich Village. The commemoration of this event turned into the first annual Pride parade, an event that celebrates inclusivity and a positive stance against discrimination. These marches now happen all across the globe, with one of the largest and most famous being the Sydney Gay and Lesbian Mardi Gras.

FUN FACT

THE ORIGINAL DESIGNER OF THE RAINBOW FLAG, ARTIST GILBERT BAKER, MADE A MILE-LONG VERSION OF THE FLAG FOR THE 25TH ANNIVERSARY OF THE STONEWALL RIOTS.

The rainbow flag, also known as the gay pride flag, has become a recognisable symbol of the movement, with the colours reflecting the diversity of the community. It's considered an inclusive and happy symbol of the movement.

Generally, Millennials tend to be supportive of LGBTQIA+ rights, such as marriage equality. They are especially invested in correcting the discriminatory motivations of others, and promoting peace and goodwill. This generation has made significant progress in encouraging the acceptance and understanding of LGBTQIA+, and the legalisation of gay marriage in more countries.

'THE ONLY QUEER PEOPLE ARE THOSE WHO DON'T LOVE ANYBODY.'

Rita Mae Brown, activist and writer

Marriage

DESPITE the trend among Millennials towards less traditional relationships, marriage continues to exist as a social structure that many aspire to. In 2018, the strength of the 'yes' vote in Australia's gay marriage referendum, and the many weddings that were held in the months following the change in law, demonstrated the importance of marriage to many Millennials.

Traditional family or religious pressures have long played their part in keeping the institution as a relevant part of life. The trend is for Millennials to reject those pressures, claiming their relationships are not in need of external validation. Increasingly, they regard marriage as an option rather than a necessity. This is demonstrated by steadily dropping marriage rates: in 1997, the number of marriages per 1000 people was 5.8, and by 2017 it had dropped to 4.6. Millennials are also likely to marry later: the median age for marriage in 1997 was 29.7 for men and 27.5 for women but by 2017 it had risen to 32.0 for men and 30.1 for women.[1]

There are many aspects at play in explaining these figures. One of these is greater gender equality: today's women are more likely to have degrees and careers than in previous generations, leaving less room for the traditional female gender role of homemaker. Another factor is that Millennials are under pressure to focus on their careers and financial futures, especially early in their working lives.

By waiting longer to commit to exclusive long-term partnerships, Millennials open themselves up to an array of life experiences. Consequently, they establish a robust individual identity prior to marriage – they have more financial stability, professional success, emotional development and self-awareness. They may well also open themselves up to a number of different relationships before they commit, so that they enter marriage on a strong developmental footing in comparison to their parents' and grandparents' generations.

Whatever the explanation, the divorce rate (the number of divorces granted per 1000 people) is dropping – from 2.8 in 1997 to 2.0 in 2017.[2]

FUN FACT

MILLENNIALS ARE MUCH MORE LIKELY TO COHABIT BEFORE GETTING MARRIED – WHILE IN 1997 65% OF PEOPLE MARRIED AFTER A PERIOD OF COHABITATION, IN 2017 THAT FIGURE WAS OVER 80%.

'MARRIAGE USED TO BE THE FIRST STEP INTO ADULTHOOD. NOW IT IS OFTEN THE LAST. FOR MANY COUPLES, MARRIAGE IS SOMETHING YOU DO WHEN YOU HAVE THE WHOLE REST OF YOUR PERSONAL LIFE IN ORDER. THEN YOU BRING FAMILY AND FRIENDS TOGETHER TO CELEBRATE.'

Andrew Cherlin, sociologist, author of Public and Private Families

Religion

OVER time, religion is losing its appeal for the Millennial generation. In the last census, the declaration of 'no religion' was particularly evident among this age group, with nearly 39% of Australians between 18 and 34 declaring that they weren't allied to any religion in 2016.[1] Barely half of this generation believe in God, and another third are uncertain.[2]

What can be seen historically as the two broad functions of religion are becoming less and less relevant to Millennials. Firstly, religion used to be relied upon to provide a moral code and a structure to deal with complex issues, such as sexuality, abortion, contraception, adultery and divorce. Millennials, however, have challenged existing standards. Educational and scientific advances, too, have brought into question certain long-held religious world views. As societal attitudes have broadened, organised religion hasn't adapted quickly enough to match the change. For example, research in the UK reports many young people are turning their backs on formally organised religious communities that seem incapable

> **FUN FACT**
>
> IN 2017, CIVIL CELEBRANTS CARRIED OUT 78% OF ALL MARRIAGES (AND 99% OF ALL SAME-SEX MARRIAGES IN THE FIRST SIX MONTHS OF 2018).

of according women full dignity, or recognising or celebrating love among LGBTQIA+ people.[3]

Secondly, religion traditionally provides a sense of community. Coinciding with the failure of organised religion to adapt to changing social mores, Millennials have become less interested in involving themselves with large-scale community organisations. Instead, they favour links with smaller social associations that are more relevant to them. They may, for instance, play in a local sports team or be a regular at a local pub trivia night. On top of the time Millennials spend on social media interacting with their online communities, they are also dealing with higher rates of university attendance, rising emphasis on work, group housing and more complicated relationship dynamics, all of which have grown to fill the gap previously occupied by religion.

When Millennials do identify with a religion – for instance by becoming members of faith traditions such as Islam, Hinduism and Buddhism – they tend to take their religion seriously.

'THE PICTURE WE SEE AMONG GEN Y
IS SMALL, INTERESTING POCKETS OF
RELIGIOUS VITALITY, BUT ON THE WHOLE,
THEY ARE A GENERATION FOR WHOM
RELIGIOUS FAITH DOES NOT RATE AS
PARTICULARLY IMPORTANT.'

Andrew Singleton, Australian sociologist of religion

Politics

O N a broad political spectrum, Australians have traditionally defined themselves as either left or right. Millennials engage very differently with politics, with many struggling to identify with a particular political party or set of policies. Neither of the traditional parties seem to fully deliver what these voters want, and they are often seeking a more participatory democracy centred on a push towards more issues-based voting. With this generation now accounting for more than a third of all voters, they can wield significant power.

FUN FACT

ACCORDING TO A 2018 DELOITTE SURVEY, 63% OF AUSTRALIAN MILLENNIALS BELIEVE POLITICIANS HAVE A NEGATIVE IMPACT ON SOCIETY. ONLY 23% SAY THEY HAVE A POSITIVE IMPACT.

Disillusioned with political point scoring, they are also more focused on the ways in which they can actively pursue change. The increase in information and choices available to them has been instrumental in the rise of activist movements such as GetUp! and Change.org, which make use of the internet and social media to connect otherwise disparate individuals. These organisations are very successful in rallying

Millennials (and others) around issues and agendas that appeal to them, forming groups that appear to be cohesive and effective.

Since time immemorial, though, idealistic younger generations have tended to be drawn to the more progressive, left side of politics. As Millennials move into positions of power, we may well see an increased propensity for intervention in the economy and support for a rise in the nation's social services investment.[1]

In general, political satisfaction and trust have dropped dramatically among this generation, and observers have no expectation that these issues will be solved soon. As Millennials influence rises, expect to see some changes!

'MAINSTREAM POLITICS OFTEN IGNORES
YOUNGER VOTERS ON ISSUES AND ON
COMMUNICATIONS AND THEN WONDERS
WHY AND COMPLAINS ABOUT THE FACT
THAT THEY APPEAR DISENGAGED.'

George Wright, former ALP National Secretary

LIFESTYLE

Drugs

WHEN it comes to drugs, people in their 20s and early 30s are more likely to drink alcohol in risky quantities and use cannabis, ecstasy or cocaine than any other age group. Sociologists have found, however, that Millennials embrace risk less enthusiastically than their 1960s counterparts, with their wild youth culture of exploring alternate states of consciousness. Rates of daily smoking, risky drinking and the use of cannabis and ecstasy are all significantly lower for Millennials than for previous generations at the same age.

The majority of recreational drugs are highly regulated, and an issue that resonates with this generation is the push for the legalisation of marijuana. It's generally considered to be less dangerous than alcohol, and as a first step there's strong support for dropping penalties for possession or use, with over 70% of Australians in favour.

Over 80% also support the use of cannabis for medicinal purposes. While this is available in Australia, it remains difficult to access in practice. Increasing numbers of Millennials agree with legalising cannabis, following a growing global trend (cannabis is legal in Canada, Uruguay and many states in the USA).[1]

A second issue that has become important to this generation is support for pill testing (or drug checking, as it is known in the northern hemisphere), a strategy that many Australian political leaders currently oppose. This is a harm prevention intervention which provides feedback to users on the content of illegal drugs, allowing them to make informed choices as to whether to take them or not. It has been shown that pill testing can affect the black market and the supply of unsafe drugs, as well as change the consumption choices of those who have their drugs tested.[2]

FUN FACT

AN ESTIMATED 70% OF ECSTASY PILLS ARE TAKEN AT CLUBS, FESTIVALS AND DANCE PARTIES.

While harm reduction strategies like this may increase risks for some (who choose not to use the service, or ignore the results), it is generally thought that it is a positive measure which could prevent deaths, and is supported by 63% of voters.[3]

In general, Millennials' attitude towards drugs fits with their more socially progressive views, with a 'live and let live' perspective. While they might not choose to partake themselves, they're unlikely to object strongly if others decide to do so.

'REJECTING PILL TESTING ON IDEOLOGICAL, OR WORSE, ON A POLITICAL BASIS AND REFUSING TO LISTEN TO THE MAJORITY OF AUSTRALIANS SEEMS LIKE GIVING UP ON OUR KIDS. PRETENDING THAT YOU CAN STOP KIDS TAKING DRUGS IS NOT ONLY NAIVE – IT'S DANGEROUS. IT'S TIME FOR A NEW WAY FORWARD AND WE HAVE THE EVIDENCE TO BACK US.'

Matt Noffs, Harm Reduction Australia

Feminism

FEMINISM – the general aim of which is to achieve equality of the sexes – is an issue with a long history. Its various campaigns, characterised as coming in waves, have led to major societal changes in many, but not all, corners of the world.

The first wave, in the early 20th century, resulted in women's right to vote in some countries, while the second wave, in the 1960s, was associated with the women's liberation movement, campaigning for legal and social equality and an end to gender discrimination. The third wave began in the 1990s and was a reaction to the perceived failures of the second wave, which was felt to have over-emphasised the experiences of upper-middle-class white women. This time it was more about challenging established social norms, questioning and redefining ideas about womanhood, gender, beauty, sexuality, femininity and masculinity. Derogatory language was reclaimed, and women were redefined as assertive, powerful and in control of their own sexuality.

The fourth wave, driven by Millennials, builds on the gains of the past but addresses sexual harassment, body shaming and rape culture, using social media to highlight and address concerns around these topics. This new technologically amplified wave has ricocheted around the globe, galvanised by high-profile incidents. One such incident was the brutal gang-rape of a young woman in India in 2012, whose subsequent death led to international outrage. Another was Donald Trump's defeat of Hillary Clinton in the 2016 US Presidential election; his inflammatory remarks about women led to mass demonstrations across the USA and around the world, known as the Women's March.

Arguably the most significant development is the Me Too movement, launched in the USA in 2006 to assist survivors of sexual violence, especially females of colour from low-wealth communities. Victims of sexual assault and harassment began sharing their experiences on social media, using the hashtag #metoo. Among the individuals named multiple times as harassers, abusers and sexual predators was Hollywood mogul Harvey Weinstein. Such is the nature of celebrity that when well-known actresses publicly added to the chorus, within days his career was destroyed. Police charges soon followed, and photos of Weinstein in handcuffs flashed around the world. Other powerful men in politics, entertainment, business and the media have subsequently been named and shamed, their reputations unlikely ever to recover, even if the expensive lawyers they retain manage to keep them out of jail.

There are concerns that Me Too has become a witchhunt. Undeniably, men everywhere are on notice that women are no longer prepared to put up with unwanted sexual advances.

'WELCOME TO THE FOURTH WAVE OF FEMINISM. WHAT'S HAPPENING NOW FEELS LIKE SOMETHING NEW AGAIN. IT'S DEFINED BY TECHNOLOGY: TOOLS THAT ARE ALLOWING WOMEN TO BUILD A STRONG, POPULAR, REACTIVE MOVEMENT ONLINE. JUST HOW POPULAR IS SOMETIMES SLIGHTLY STARTLING.'

Kira Cochrane, British writer and women's rights advocate

Housing

To large numbers of Millennials, the 'Great Australian Dream' of owning your own home appears to be permanently out of reach. Investigating why this should be, one recent study cited 'economic constraints, lifestyle choices and work–home preferences'[1], implying that Millennials are pricing themselves out of the market by choosing to spend money on higher rents to live a better lifestyle and be closer to work. In other words, they're not exercising the delayed gratification required to save up for a deposit.

But that judgement is somewhat unfair if you consider the other factors at play. Housing affordability in Australia has steadily declined, while the demand for sustainable, affordable housing continues to grow. This has put pressure on prices, particularly for those in the low-income bracket. In fact, the property market has grown at a rate above inflation for the last ten years while wage growth has been minimal. The relative cost of entering the housing market has made it unachievable for many, except those counting on 'The Bank of Mum and Dad'.

Millennials also carry significantly higher levels of debt than did previous generations, largely driven by the increase in university enrolment and the associated student loans; admittedly, Australian students are insulated from the full effect, thanks to the government HECS/HELP scheme. Yet Millennials also face increased need for tertiary qualifications to access the current job market. Further, in order to access that job market, young people are forced into cities, where housing is generally more expensive.

Given Australia's thriving investment economy, this situation is likely to continue, hence there will be more apartment buildings and concentrated city living. In turn, this will require a rethink on the services and amenities that need to be provided.

FUN FACT

IN 1981, THE COST OF A FLIGHT TO LONDON WOULD HAVE BEEN $9452 IN TODAY'S ECONOMY, WHILE A 20% DEPOSIT ON A MEDIAN-PRICED HOUSE IN SYDNEY WAS $60,809. TODAY, THAT FLIGHT TO LONDON COSTS $1300, AND AS YOUR 20% DEPOSIT FOR A MEDIAN-PRICE HOUSE IN SYDNEY YOU'D NEED $206,778.

In the meantime, falling rates of home ownership and rising rent costs have changed the way Millennials live. Co-living spaces with individual studios or bedrooms but with shared communal spaces and luxury amenities are growing in popularity, often with other perks, such as organised group events and weekly housekeeping.

'BY FAILING TO ADDRESS HOUSING AFFORDABILITY, PRIORITISING INVESTORS AND ALLOWING RATES OF FOREIGN OWNERSHIP TO RISE – THE GOVERNMENT IS SELLING OUT YOUNG AUSTRALIANS, AND OUR PARENTS ARE LETTING THEM. THE GENERATION THAT HAD EVERYTHING GOING FOR THEM HAS TURNED THEIR BACK ON MILLENNIALS, AND RUBBED SALT INTO THE WOUND, BY TELLING US TO "TOUGHEN UP".'

Megan Shellie, intergenerational fairness advocate

The New Sharing Economy

MILLENNIALS have led the push to both develop and use a sharing economy – one in which peer-to-peer sharing of goods and services is carried out by way of online transactions. The starting point for the idea was that expensive items tend to be owned by people who don't make full use of them; so why not develop the technology for people to be able to rent things more easily from each other? Access could trump ownership, with both owners and users benefiting – owners making money from underutilised assets and users paying less than they might otherwise. This also fit well with growing anti-consumerism sentiment coupled with the desire for a more environmentally sustainable lifestyle.

Companies sprang up to service this economy, acting not as the actual service provider but as the facilitator to make the transaction happen. That could be finding a driver to take you to your destination (Uber, founded in 2009), renting a room when travelling (Airbnb, founded in 2008) or providing a platform to sell unwanted goods (eBay, founded in 1995). These used technology such as smartphones with global positioning system (GPS) locators and online payment systems, and built credence through online reviews and ratings.

A feature of these companies is that they enable ordinary individuals to start a business – or at least a 'side hustle', or additional income stream. It is both easy and potentially lucrative to participate in this collaborative economy. The flip side, however, is that self-employed individuals usually forgo work stability and employee benefits in exchange for work flexibility.

In parallel with the growth of the sharing economy, a 'gig economy' has developed, whereby businesses contract individual workers for short-term engagements. At best, this model is powered by independent workers choosing the jobs they accept. At worst, it is a curse for young workers forced to live without either employee benefits or certainty: unable to gain permanent employment, they take temporary gigs to cover their living costs. The gig economy is a feature of today's workplace, with its digital connectivity, never-ending, technology-driven change in job roles and the financial pressures on businesses.

'AS PEOPLE'S ACCESS TO THE INTERNET
GROWS WE'RE SEEING THE SHARING
ECONOMY BOOM — I THINK OUR OBSESSION
WITH OWNERSHIP IS AT A TIPPING POINT
AND THE SHARING ECONOMY IS PART OF
THE ANTIDOTE FOR THAT.'

Richard Branson, business magnate

Climate Change

THE environment is front of mind for Millennials, who are deeply concerned about the impact that climate change will have on future generations. They tend to be particularly unimpressed by climate-change deniers – especially those in government positions – and the lack of government efforts to tackle the environmental challenges the world is facing.

Millennials have observed political will on this issue build, only to drop off. There was a clear environmental focus in the 1990s, with the UN Earth Summit in 1992 bringing together over 100 heads of state to set goals and declare their intentions to save the earth. But positive action was slow, and despite a growing body of evidence on vanishing habitats, waning energy resources and global warming, green issues lost ground to the global focus on fighting terrorism after 9/11. Among the small steps taken since are the 1997 Kyoto Protocol (to reduce carbon dioxide emissions and greenhouse gases) and the 2015 Paris Agreement (to strengthen the global response to the threat of climate change) – both non-binding – and many countries have failed to meet their targets or withdrawn completely.

Despite some of our leading politicians still discrediting the science, Millennials are under no illusion about the threats that global warming poses. Australia is particularly vulnerable to climate change: the climate has warmed by one degree since 1910, the Great Barrier Reef is dying amid rising ocean temperatures, and bushfire seasons are becoming longer and more intense.

Perhaps the biggest catch for Australia is that the economy benefits significantly from the country's status as the world's largest coal exporter. Consequently, big mining companies wield power and there is ongoing political inaction. It's no wonder that Millennials doubt that purposeful action will ever take place: in the last decade, they've seen three prime ministers lose their jobs, none of them able to resolve climate policy turmoil within their respective parties.

FUN FACT

THE LOWY INSTITUTE SURVEY OF 2018 FOUND THAT NEARLY 60% OF AUSTRALIANS CONSIDER GLOBAL WARMING A SERIOUS AND PRESSING PROBLEM AND THAT STEPS SHOULD BE TAKEN TO TRY AND SOLVE IT, EVEN IF IT INVOLVES SIGNIFICANT COST.

Recent government approval for a new coal mine – Australia's largest ever – reaffirms Australia's pro-coal stance. This project – which entails large-scale dredging of the seabed near the Great Barrier Reef Marine Park, the generation of 4.7 billion tonnes of greenhouse gas emissions and an unrestricted licence to use groundwater from the Great Artesian basin – only compounds the concerns that this generation has for the future of Australia and the planet.

'IT'S INCREDIBLY HARD TO DESCRIBE HOW UTTERLY SAD IT FEELS TO BE A SCIENTIST AND DAD IN A COUNTRY BEING DICTATED TO BY A SMALL GROUP OF SCIENCE-DENYING CLOWNS PUTTING THEIR OWN SHORT-TERM POLITICAL GAIN OVER THE LONG-TERM PUBLIC INTEREST.'

Dr Darren Saunders, cancer biologist and science media contributor

Education

MILLENNIALS have seen considerable change in tertiary education, both in its accessibility and delivery. But have the outcomes been positive?

On one hand, Millennials are the beneficiaries of government policy to open up access to university for wider numbers than ever before, especially minority groups. Between 2009 and 2018, rates of attendance at tertiary level rose by 89% for Indigenous students, 52% for those from low socio-economic backgrounds and 47% for those from regional and remote areas.[1] However, when federal funding became based largely on student numbers, this created an incentive for universities to increase enrolments – and in many cases this has come at the expense of academic skills. Unfortunately, this resulted in falling graduation rates and academic standards.

The jump in numbers of people accessing universities has resulted in 'education inflation', or the devaluing of a first degree, which has become a basic requirement for a much wider range of jobs than previously. This has led to growth in the number of highly qualified graduates looking for jobs, giving employers less incentive to compete, and putting pressure on starting salaries. In their efforts to stand out in the workplace, many Millennials are obtaining further qualifications, such as masters degrees.

In parallel with these developments, tertiary tuition fees have risen worldwide, and consequently

Millennials are often significantly in debt before they start working. While in Australia the system of government loans is workable – only increasing by the cost of living, and with repayments made directly through the taxation system once a threshold of earning is reached – in countries such as the USA, private loans can saddle students with crippling debt.

FUN FACT

IN 2017, JUST UNDER 27% OF PEOPLE IN AUSTRALIA HAVE A BACHELOR-LEVEL DEGREE OR HIGHER QUALIFICATION, UP FROM 15% IN 2000 AND JUST 5% IN 1976.

Debt means that many students are forced into working while learning, spurring significant changes to teaching practices, such as the timing and delivery of classes and online and short courses. Once again, the development of technology has made this possible, and allows this tech-savvy generation to be more engaged in their learning in that new portable learning environment.

There are also plenty of options for Millennials who want to pick up skills without committing to formal education. Courses, often self-paced and accessed at will online, are available from providers such as the Khan Academy, and TEDx talks also attract a large Millennial audience.

'WITH SO MANY HIGHLY QUALIFIED GRADUATES AFTER THE SAME JOB, EMPLOYERS HAVE LESS INCENTIVE TO COMPETE BY OFFERING HIGHER STARTING SALARIES. THOSE GRADUATES WHO MISS OUT ON THE BEST JOBS WILL FIND WORK, BUT THIS MIGHT BE A TEACHING GRADUATE WORKING IN A CHILDCARE CENTRE, OR A LAW GRADUATE DRIVING AN UBER.'

Brian Redican, Chief Economist at NSW Treasury Corporation

Working Life

WHEN it comes to employment, Millennials are often portrayed as a lazy generation, overly self-confident and requiring constant positive affirmation – none of which is supported by evidence. For their part, Millennials see themselves as educated, curious, connected, flexible and innovative, with much to offer potential employers. This is the group that will make up 75% of the global workforce by 2025, so it's important to understand their motivations.

On the issue of finding employment, the changing nature of work is creating barriers for this generation. Structural changes in the economy have hit the lower end of the job market: economists cite influences like the globalised nature of the economy, the rapid pace of technological change – particularly automation – and an increased casualisation of the workforce. Real-world effects include suppressed wages and conditions for those at the bottom of the pay scale, and a tendency towards an unpaid work culture, for example, in the form of internships sought by students wishing to build up experience in order to transition from education to the workplace.

For Millennials who land permanent employment, while they're attracted by good pay and positive corporate culture, they're looking for more in a workplace. The keys to keeping them loyal and happy are flexibility and diversity – a workplace that values tolerance, inclusiveness, openness, respect and different ways of thinking. They also want to work with companies that put effort into training them and developing their skills, rather than companies solely focused on profits and unwilling to share financial rewards with their workers. They seek out close relationships with their bosses, looking for them to be mentor, confidant and friend as well as leader.

FUN FACT

MILLENNIALS FEEL NEGATIVELY ABOUT THE MOTIVATIONS AND OPINIONS OF THE BUSINESS SECTOR. ONLY 48% BELIEVE THAT CORPORATIONS BEHAVE ETHICALLY, AND NEARLY 40% BELIEVE THAT BUSINESS LEADERS ARE HAVING A NEGATIVE IMPACT ON THE WORLD.

Their familiarity with technology makes Millennials well placed to suggest innovative ways to improve the businesses in which they're involved, especially in operations and marketing roles. Even so, many doubt their preparedness to deal with workplace changes associated with the so-called Industry 4.0 revolution – in which artificial intelligence, cognitive computing and analytics will feature heavily – and are relying on their employers to help them adapt.

If companies fail to meet Millennials' expectations, Millannials are liable to turn to the gig economy. For many, it is an attractive and viable alternative to full-time employment. Those who view it positively talk up its potential for delivering higher earnings, flexibility and freedom in both senior and junior roles. According to reputable surveys, 70% of this generation have, or want to have, their own business.

'MILLENNIALS ARE MORE AWARE OF SOCIETY'S MANY CHALLENGES THAN PREVIOUS GENERATIONS AND LESS WILLING TO ACCEPT MAXIMIZING SHAREHOLDER VALUE AS A SUFFICIENT GOAL FOR THEIR WORK. THEY ARE LOOKING FOR A BROADER SOCIAL PURPOSE AND WANT TO WORK SOMEWHERE THAT HAS SUCH A PURPOSE.'

Michael Porter, author of Competitive Advantage

Travel

E NABLED by their technological connections, Millennials consider themselves as citizens of the world, and this affects both their attitudes to travel and to the political issue of immigration.

Travel plays a very important role in the lives of Millennials, and they have an enthusiastic desire to immerse themselves in other places and cultures as travellers. At any given time, close to three quarters of all Millennials have the intention to take a holiday in the next 12 months, higher than any other generation; they're also the most likely group to take a short break.[1] Their preference is to spend the money they earn on experiences over things, which means that they lust after fresh adventures: 29% of Millennials are most interested in recommendations that expose them to something new.

FUN FACT

OVER HALF OF MILLENNIALS CONSIDER SOCIAL MEDIA POSTS WHEN CHOOSING A HOTEL, AND 56% USE FACEBOOK THE MOST FOR SHARING THEIR HOLIDAY SNAPS.

Technology has facilitated the discovery and sharing of these experiences. Millennials are adept at comparing options using digital tools, sourcing reviews and recommendations from fellow travellers, booking travel online, and sharing their experiences through social media apps. As well, Millennials lead the way in using sharing economy services for trip accommodation (Airbnb), and accessing ride-sharing apps when they travel (Uber), with 45% of Australian Millennials using these services.

Millennial travellers are also environmentally and socially aware: they've grown up with recycling as a norm and are attuned to social-justice issues. They want to minimise the harm they do to the environment and actually meet the people who live in the places they're visiting. This has led to the development of more sustainable travel options which benefit local communities and offer more authentic experiences, such as travelling on local public transport and using a local guide.

An interest in engaging with other cultures goes hand in hand with fostering empathy and cross-cultural understanding, and this applies in day-to-day life as well as when travelling. This generation tends to be both accepting of cultural differences at home and welcoming of immigrants and asylum seekers.

Then again, immigration has featured more in their lives than is the case for earlier generations. This generation has the largest number of individuals who identify as multiracial: close to one in three Australian Millennials has been born in Asia.

'THEY WANT DIFFERENT EXPERIENCES IN TRAVEL, SO THE INDUSTRY MUST SERVE THEM DIFFERENTLY. TRAVEL PROVIDERS WILL NEED TO ADOPT NEW TECHNOLOGY, NEW STRATEGIES, AND ABOVE ALL, NEW MINDSETS IF THEY WANT TO SECURE MILLENNIAL MIND AND MARKET SHARE.'

Karun Budhraja, leading marketer in the travel industry

Language – in Short!

ILLENNIALS are adept at rapid online communication. Their ability to use both hands to key and not drop their handheld device is astonishing, and they also use cleverly abbreviated language and graphics, such as emojis, to speed things up. Smartphones have tiny screens, and the goal is to convey as much meaning as possible using as few characters as you can so that recipients can take in their messages at a glance, eg while at work. Restrictions like Twitter's original limit of 140 characters per message provided the impetus to condense language.

Internet shorthand is continually evolving but abbreviations like btw (capitals optional), meaning 'by the way', seem to have become staples.

af - as f*** (a lot)
bae - before anything else
bff - best friend forever
bf - boyfriend
brb - be right back
btw - by the way
cbf - can't be f***ed
dm - direct message
fb - Facebook
ffs - for f***'s sake
fomo - fear of missing out
ftw - for the win (the best!)
gf - girlfriend
gtfo - get the f*** out
hbu - how about you?
icymi - in case you missed it
idc - I don't care

idk - I don't know
ig - Instagram
ikr - I know right?
ily - I love you
imo - in my opinion
irl - in real life
jks - jokes (joking!)
lmao - laughing my arse off
lol - laugh out loud
nvm - never mind
nsfw - not safe for work
og - original gangster (the first)
omg - oh my God
omw - on my way
plz - please
rn - right now
rofl - rolling on the floor laughing
smh - shaking my head
stfu - shut the f*** up
tbh - to be honest
tbt - throw back to
tfw - that feeling when
tl;dr - too long; didn't read
tmi - too much information
ttyl - talk to you later
wdym - what do you mean?
wtf - what the f***
wyd - what you doing?
yolo - you only live once

Another approach is to abbreviate words to one or two syllables and cut off the rest, as in totes (totally), perf (perfect), jelly (jealous) or feels (feelings).

Becoming adept at using internet language won't necessarily put you on the same footing as a Millennial. Take 'lol', for instance. Since the expression went mainstream, Millennials have tended to say it in an ironic way, finding it humorous when others use the term seriously.

Help is always available from online resources such as urban dictionary, which explains not only meanings for new terms – such as mansplaining (when a man explains something to a woman she already understands and he does so in a patronising way) or manspreading (when a man sits next to you with his legs wide apart, encroaching on your personal space), but also the finer points of usage.

FUN FACT

'LIT' CAN DESCRIBE A SITUATION OR EVENT THAT'S EXTREMELY COOL, EXCITING OR CRAZY, EG 'THIS PARTY IS SO FREAKING LIT RIGHT NOW.' HIP-HOP ARTIST TRAVIS SCOTT FREQUENTLY INTERSPERSES 'IT'S LIT' WITH LYRICS ON SONGS HE PRODUCES.

Graphics and visual language also feature heavily, which reflects the universality and efficiency of the visual. Although much of the technology driving the internet was developed in the Silicon Valley of the USA, using American English, billions of users are non-native speakers. Visuals can convey emotion and dynamism, be playful and creative. Emoticons such as the happy face, the cry-laughing face, the kiss heart, the thinking face and the sad face can introduce a tone that the words alone don't convey. These and every emotion in between are easily accessed via the keyboard of any mobile phone and are readily used by Millennials to punctuate their communications.

'TECHNOLOGY AND THE INTERNET HAS ACCELERATED THE EVOLUTION OF LANGUAGE. I DON'T THINK IT'S A SEPARATE LANGUAGE, BUT THE INTERNET HAS DEFINITELY SPED UP THE CHANGES IN ENGLISH.'

Aaron Peckham, founder of Urban Dictionary

Gen Z

So, who comes after the Millennials? For individuals born between 1995 and 2009, the answer is Gen Z. What's next is Gen Alpha, and they're still a work in progress: watch this space.

Mostly the children of Gen X parents, Gen-Zers are the largest generation ever, making up 20% of Australia's population and almost 30% of the world's population. Globally, there are two billion of them!

The distinguishing feature of Gen-Zers is that they've been born post the internet. They are digital integrators – the first fully global generation to grow up with technology as an integrated part of their lives – fully connected through digital devices and engaged through social media. This is why they've also been called 'generation connected', 'iGen' and 'dot.com kids'. On average, members of this generation use their smartphones for 15.4 hours per week – more than any other device – but additionally have several screens at their disposal.[1]

As digital dependence has grown, so too has cyber bullying: it now looms large as a serious issue, with a third of children reporting having been bullied via social networking websites, instant messaging, text or email.[2] The incidence of anxiety is also on the rise. Recent studies show this generation is recording the highest incidence of depression, anxiety and sleep disturbance.[3]

They have also grown up in the shadow of two major events – 9/11 and the resulting war on terrorism, and the global financial crisis – although they may be only vaguely aware of either occurrence. Their parents, however, have had to adjust to phenomena such as higher levels of state surveillance, financial stress, a growing income gap between rich and poor, and a shrinking middle class. Education, therefore, is seen as vital for this generation, and they are the most formally educated generation in history – with more institutions to choose from and more ways to study than ever before. However, they will also incur more study debt than any other generation in history.[4]

FUN FACT

GEN Z ARE FOLLOWED BY GEN ALPHA, THOSE BORN FROM 2010, AND THERE ARE 2,500,000 OF THEM BORN GLOBALLY EACH WEEK. HOWEVER, BY 2034, WHEN THEY HIT THEIR EARLY 20s, FOR THE FIRST TIME IN OUR HISTORY, THERE WILL BE MORE AUSTRALIANS AGED OVER 60 THAN UNDER 20.

Gen Z has outstanding multitasking skills – able to move quickly from one task to another with more value on speed than accuracy. They will also be the most empowered generation and will be entering the workforce at a time when more people are leaving it than entering it.[5] It has been predicted that, on average, a member of Generation Z will work 17 jobs, have 5 careers, and live in 15 homes in their lifetime.[6]

'(GEN Z) ARE PERHAPS THE MOST BRAND-CRITICAL, BULLSHIT-REPELLENT, QUESTIONING GROUP AROUND AND WILL CALL OUT ANY BEHAVIOR THEY DISLIKE ON SOCIAL MEDIA.'

Lucie Green, British science communicator and solar researcher

---

Notes

INTRODUCTION

1. Struebi, Patrick, 'A New Zeitgeist Has Arrived. Are You Part of It?', huffingtonpost.com, updated 24 September 2016

MILLENNIALS

1. Strauss, William and Howe, Neil, *Millennials Rising: The Next Great Generation*, Vintage, New York, 2000
2. time.com/247/millennials-the-me-me-me-generation

FACEBOOK

1. Osnos, Evan, 'Can Mark Zuckerberg Fix Facebook Before It Breaks Democracy?', newyorker.com, 10 September 2018
2. journalism.org/2015/06/01/millennials-political-news/ Pew Center Research

ECHO CHAMBERS

1. independent.co.uk/voices/donald-trump-president-social-media-echo-chamber-hypernormalisation-adam-curtis-protests-blame-a7409481.html

YOUTUBE

1. mediakix.com/2018/03/top-influencers-social-media-instagram-youtube

STREAMING

1. statista.com/statistics/896078/australia-streaming-services-by-type/
2. forbes.com/sites/andrewarnold/2017/11/15/5-reasons-why-millennials-lead-other-generations-in-podcast-consumption

(LACK OF) ONLINE PRIVACY

1. See for example, 'Privacy and Human Rights: An International Survey of Privacy Laws and Practice' by Privacy International at http://gilc.org/privacy/survey/intro.html
2. duckduckgo.com/
3. www.eff.org/

AMAZON

1. theatlantic.com/business/archive/2014/05/amazon-has-basically-no-competition-among-online-booksellers/371917/

BITCOIN AND BLOCKCHAIN

1. nytimes.com/2017/10/01/technology/what-is-bitcoin-price.html

SELF-BRAND

1. (Berrett-Koehler Publishers, San Francisco, various editions)

'IT'S COMPLICATED' RELATIONSHIPS

1. abs.gov.au/ausstats/abs@.nsf/Lookup/by%20Subject/2071.0~2016~Main%20Features~Same-Sex%20Couples~85
2. news.gallup.com/poll/183515/fewer-young-people-say-relationship.aspx

MARRIAGE

1. All 1997 statistics are taken from Australian Bureau of Statistics, Marriages and Divorces, Australia, 1997; 2017 statistics are from Australian Bureau of Statistics, Marriages and Divorces, Australia, 2017
2. Ibid.

RELIGION

1. abs.gov.au/ausstats/abs@.nsf/Lookup/by%20
Subject/2071.0~2016~Main%20Features~Religion%20
Data%20Summary~70
2. Singleton, A., 'Generations of Change: Religion and
Spirituality in Contemporary Australia', LiNQ, Vol. 38, Dec
2011: 110–115.
3. theconversation.com/how-religion-rises-and-falls-in-modern-
australia-74367

POLITICS

1. Switzer, T. and Jacobs, C., 'Millennials and socialism:
Australian youth are lurching to the left', The Centre for
Independent Studies Policy Paper No. 7, June 2018

DRUGS

1. National Drug Strategy Household Survey 2016
aihw.gov.au/getmedia/15db8c15-7062-4cde-bfa4-
3c2079f30af3/21028a.pdf.aspx?inline=true
2. drugpolicy.org.au/pill_testing?gclid=EAIaIQobChMIkuWdyv
bd4QIVDBWPCh3l0Q-oEAAYASAAEgIhPfD_BwE
3. theguardian.com/australia-news/2019/jan/15/overwhelming-
majority-of-voters-support-pill-testing-guardian-essential-poll

HOUSING

1. aihw.gov.au/reports/housing-assistance/housing-assistance-
in-australia-2018/contents/housing-in-australia

EDUCATION

1. docs.education.gov.au/system/files/doc/other/2018_first_half_year_higher_education_student_summary_time_series.pdf

TRAVEL

1. roymorgan.com/findings/7603-millennials-plan-to-travel-more-than-other-australians-201805250640

2. scdn.thomascook.com/images/wcms/dam/tcuk/campaigns/campaigns2018/holidayreport2018/TCookHolidayReport2018.pdf?_ga=2.63180589.344687493.1526292078-1291724249.1525879342

GEN Z

1. visioncritical.com/generation-z-infographics/

2. mccrindle.com.au/insights/blogarchive/generation-z-defined-global-visual-digital/

3. geneticsofdepression.org.au/poor-report-card-for-nations-mental-health/

4. mccrindle.com.au/insights/blogarchive/generation-z-commence-university-choosing-the-right-course/

5. McCrindle, Mark, *The ABC of XYZ*, www.theabcofxyz.com; https://mccrindle.com.au/wp-content/uploads/2016/12/McCrindle-Research_ABC-03_The-Generation-Map_Mark-McCrindle.pdf

6. mccrindle.com.au/insights/blogarchive/generation-z-defined-global-visual-digital/

ACKNOWLEDGEMENTS

None of the information in this book would have seen the light of day without the challenge of raising three confident, worldly and opinionated Millennial children. They unfortunately have minds of their own, and aren't afraid to point out how Baby Boomers in general (and their parents in particular) are hopelessly out of touch.

Special thanks to Matt, studying half a world away, who took some relish in bringing me up to speed on all things Millennial. He was ever patient when I admitted I had no clue what he was talking about in our weekly conversation, and never took offence when I said, 'Are you sure that's what Millennials think and not just your weird opinion?' (Admittedly the research generally backed up whatever he said.) Thanks, too, to Rach and Dom, who added their own unique points of view on various topics, and offered endless encouragement and free technological support from wherever they happened to be in the world.

A massive thank you to the other Millennials in my life, who I am delighted and proud to call my colleagues and friends, and who were also part of the inspiration for this book. To Ali, Marty, Lex, Elly, Anna, Lucy and Kirsty, thank you for being the best workmates, and for keeping the token 'Oldie' in the office young at heart. To the Gen-Xers, Anabel and Lucy, and my fellow Oldies, Jenny and John who help balance out the Millennial angst.

And last, but by no means least, to my editor extraordinaire Anne, whose contagious enthusiasm for the subject matter and its value was inspiring, and who excelled in pulling the manuscript into what I hope is an accessible and informative read for all Oldies.

And finally to Shane. His enthusiasm, curiosity and willingness to engage with and understand people of all ages is something that our children tease him about endlessly, but has sparked not only their own journeys, but also this one of mine.

Katy McEwen is a Baby Boomer surrounded by Millennials. She grew up in the UK and has spent her life around books, including working in a bookshop and various publishing companies before moving to Australia. She now works for a young, independent publishing company as a token 'Oldie', selling the rights for Australian books to an international audience.

Married with three Millennial children she is constantly trying to understand, Katy decided that there must be others who would like to be let in on their secrets too. And so *Oldies' Guide to the Millennial World* (with some help from her kids and workmates) was born.